SEARCH, PONDER, and PLAY with

# S U P E R
# SCRIPTURE ACTIVITIES

Tell Me the Stories of Jesus

Fun-to-Make Visuals  ○  SEARCH and PONDER Cards

Show-and-Tell Presentations  ○  Games and Activities

Primary Songs  ○  Favors and Prizes  ○  Thought Treats

Scripture Activity Invitations  ○  Bonus Motivators

## TELL ME THE STORIES OF JESUS

### ACTIVITY THEMES:

**AN ANGEL TELLS OF TWO BIRTHS:**
John and Jesus

**FISHERS OF MEN:**
Jesus Chose 12 Apostles

**THE GIFTS HE GAVE:**
Tell Me the Stories of Jesus

Covenant Communications, Inc.
American Fork, Utah

Printed in the United States of America
First Printing: August 1995

95 96 97 98 99 00 01    10 9 8 7 6 5 4 3 2 1

*Super Scripture Activities:Tell Me the Stories of Jesus*

ISBN 1-55503-860-3

# INTRODUCTION

## *Tell Me the Stories of Jesus*

Too often in today's world, videos and television replace scripture reading programs, and children grow up not knowing the real stories from the scriptures. But now there's a great way to beat the competition!

In this useful and entertaining volume, you'll find New Testament activities to make learning fun.

At home or in the classroom, any day can be a scripture-reading fun day with these theme-coordinated activities. Everything is planned for you, with patterns ready to copy and enjoy. Just choose the activities that suit your individual needs, or combine activities to enjoy a SUPER SCRIPTURE ACTIVITY.

This volume offers a variety of exciting New Testament themes for your study and enjoyment. Each fun, information-filled section stimulates an interest in the scriptures, and includes activities to entertain and delight. It is designed to help children gain a testimony of Jesus Christ and learn to live as he did.

Using the materials presented here, you'll be able to choose from many activities to enhance your New Testament course of study. SEARCH and PONDER the scriptures, and then PLAY: Have fun with activities that reinforce scripture learning. Each activity helps you better understand the scriptures and make them part of your life.

**SUPPLIES ARE SIMPLE:** Pattern copies, scissors, crayons or markers, tape, glue, string, simple craft supplies, and Thought Treats

### CHOOSE FROM THE FOLLOWING ACTIVITIES AS YOU SEARCH, PONDER, AND PLAY:

## SEARCH and PONDER

- ☐ SEARCH & PONDER cards help you SEARCH the scriptures to find missing words, and PONDER scripture questions.
- ☐ SCRIPTURE SHOW-AND-TELL with pictures to color and present with cue cards.

## PLAY: SUPER SCRIPTURE ACTIVITY Choices

- ☐ SCRIPTURE SHOW-AND-TELL presentations.
- ☐ GAMES or ACTIVITIES to make learning fun.
- ☐ SONGS from the Children's Songbook* are suggested.
- ☐ FAVOR and PRIZE patterns are ready to copy, cut and paste.
- ☐ THOUGHT TREATS to sweeten the appetite for more scripture reading.
- ☐ INVITATIONS to invite guests to a SUPER SCRIPTURE ACTIVITY featuring choices above.
- ☐ BONUS MOTIVATORS to reward guests for completing the Search and Ponder cards.

*Children's Songbook, CD, and cassette tapes are published by The Church of Jesus Christ of Latter-day Saints, Salt Lake City, Utah.

# TABLE OF CONTENTS

Super Scripture Activity Theme #1

## ANGEL TELLS OF TWO BIRTHS: John and Jesus

## SEARCH and PONDER

## PLAY

# THE GIFTS HE GAVE: Tell Me the Stories of Jesus

## SEARCH and PONDER

## PLAY

→
↓

# SCRIPTURE ACTIVITY CHECKLIST
### An Angel Tells of Two Births: John and Jesus

PAGES:

The Angel Gabriel appeared to Zacharias, Mary and Joseph, telling them that John the Baptist and Jesus would be born. John would tell the people that Jesus is coming, and would baptize Jesus. Jesus would come to tell us of Heavenly Father's plan.

Did you know that John and Jesus would be cousins? John's mother, Elisabeth, and Jesus' mother, Mary, were cousins.

Let's go to a family reunion and meet the kinfolk of John and Jesus.

PAGES:

**DO AHEAD:**
- ☐ Copy patterns ... 14-25
- ☐ Create Invitation or Favor: Baby Newsletter announcing births with baby spoon . 2-4
- ☐ Gather supplies*

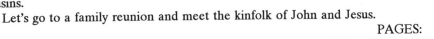

## SEARCH and PONDER:

- ☐ SEARCH & PONDER cards . . . . . . . . . . . . . . . . . . . . . . . . . 6-7
- ☐ SCRIPTURE SHOW-AND-TELL: Rehearse cue cards for presentation: Angel Tells of Two Births sack puppet show . . . . . . . . 8-11

## PLAY: SUPER SCRIPTURE ACTIVITY Choices

- ☐ SCRIPTURE SHOW-AND-TELL presentation
- ☐ GAME: Baby Spoons and Baby News Match ... 12
- ☐ SONGS:
  - ○ "I Am a Child of God," page 2**
  - ○ "He Sent His Son," page 34**
  - ○ "Little Jesus," page 38**
  - ○ "Baptism," page 100**
- ☐ FAVORS and PRIZES: . . . . . . . . . . . . . . . . . . 13
  - ○ We Love Babies medallion
  - ○ John and Jesus baby spoons
- ☐ THOUGHT TREATS: . . . . . . . . . . . . . . . . . 13-14
  - ○ Baby Love Milk with cup label
  - ○ Angel Food Cake with sign
- ☐ BONUS MOTIVATORS: . . . . . . . . . . . . . . . 24

**\*SUPPLIES:**
Pattern copies, scissors, crayons or markers, stapler, paper punch, string or ribbon, 8-ounce paper cups, and Thought Treats

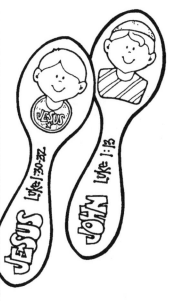

SUPPLEMENTAL READING--New Testament Stories**: Elisabeth and Zacharias, Mary and the Angel, John the Baptist is Born, Joseph and the Angel, and Jesus Christ is Born

**Children's Songbook and New Testament Stories are published by The Church of Jesus Christ of Latter-day Saints, Salt Lake City, Utah.

## INVITATION or FAVOR:  Baby Newsletter

**YOU'LL NEED** copies of the following patterns on light blue cardstock paper for each guest:
♥ Baby Newsletter pattern on page 3.
♥ Spoon invitation insert on page 4 . . . . . . . . . . . . . . . . . . IF SENDING AN INVITATION.
♥ John and Jesus baby spoon on page 5  . . IF PLAYING GAME OR USING SPOON AS FAVOR.

### HOW TO CREATE INVITATION:

1. Cut out invitation insert spoon.
2. Color in.
3. Fill in "To," "Date," "Time," and "Place" details.
4. Cut two slits in the newsletter with a razor blade  to create a pocket.
5. Insert spoon invitation in newsletter pocket.

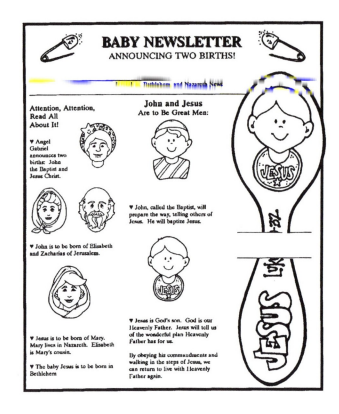

### HOW TO CREATE FAVOR:

1. Color and cut out John and Jesus baby spoon.
2. Fold and glue back-to-back.
3. Use spoon to play Baby Spoons and Baby News Match game on page 12.
4. Cut two slits in the newsletter with a razor blade to create a pocket (if not done when sending invitation).
5. Insert John and Jesus spoon in newsletter pocket.

### COLOR AHEAD OPTION:

1. Cut out and glue together one or two John and Jesus spoons for each guest.
2. Insert baby spoon(s) behind invitation spoon in newsletter pocket.
3. Instruct guests to color the spoon(s) and bring to activity to "scoop up the good news!"

# BABY NEWSLETTER
## ANNOUNCING TWO BIRTHS!

---

### Jerusalem, Bethlehem, and Nazareth News

---

**Attention, Attention, Read All About It!**

♥ Angel Gabriel announces two births: John the Baptist and Jesus Christ.

♥ John is to be born of Elisabeth and Zacharias of Jerusalem.

♥ Jesus is to be born of Mary. Mary lives in Nazareth. Elisabeth is Mary's cousin.

♥ The baby Jesus is to be born in Bethlehem.

### John and Jesus
Are to Be Great Men:

♥ John, called the Baptist, will prepare the way, telling others of Jesus. He will baptize Jesus.

♥ Jesus is God's son. God is our Heavenly Father. Jesus will tell us of the wonderful plan Heavenly Father has for us.

By obeying his commandments and walking in the steps of Jesus, we can return to live with Heavenly Father again.

---

---

**Bring newsletter to ACTIVITY to scoop up the good news!**

**PATTERN:** Baby spoon invitation insert to slide in Baby Newsletter favor  ♥ Copy on light blue cardstock paper.

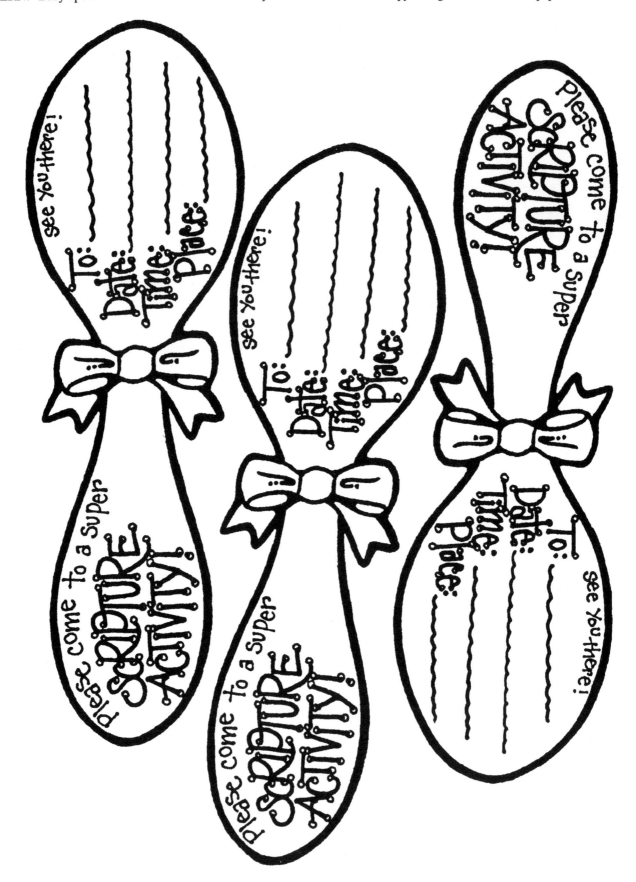

**PATTERN:** Baby spoons for Baby News Match game (two sets for each guest)  ♥ Copy on light blue cardstock paper.

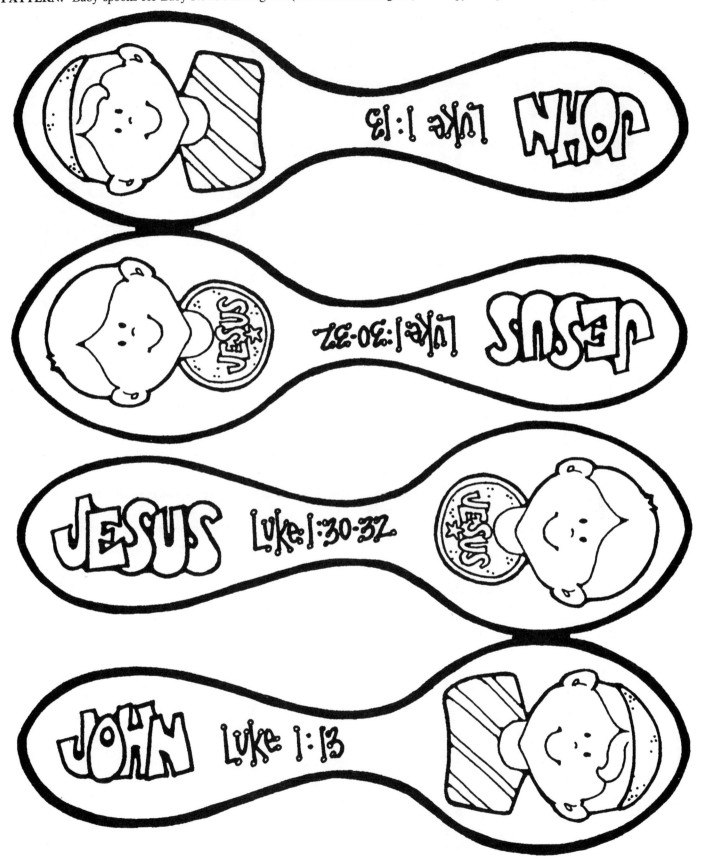

# Scripture SEARCH and PONDER:

♥ Copy one or two sets of SEARCH and PONDER cards below on colored cardstock paper.  ♥ Cut out cards.
- ◘ Use Set #1 for Daily Devotionals.
- ◘ OPTION:  Make a second set of cards to play The New Testament Game--Spotlighting the Life of Jesus.  (This is game found on pages 59-60 of SUPER SCRIPTURE ACTIVITIES--NEW TESTAMENT, by Mary H. Ross and Jennette Guymon.  Copy each set of cards a different color to identify quickly, i.e. copy this set light blue.)

## SEARCH #1
John and Jesus

**Elisabeth and Zacharias**

**Want a Baby**

"And they had no
_ _ _ _ _, because that
Elisabeth was barren, and they
both were now well stricken in
years." (Luke 1:7)

## SEARCH #2
John and Jesus

**Angel Gabriel Tells**

**Zacharias About John**

"But the angel said unto him,
Fear not, Zacharias: for thy
_ _ _ _ _ _ is heard; and
thy wife Elisabeth shall bear
thee a son, and thou shalt call
his name John." ( Luke 1:13)

## SEARCH #3
John and Jesus

**Doubting Zacharias Is Punished**

"And Zacharias said unto the
angel, Whereby shall I
_ _ _ _ _ this?  for I am
an old man, and my wife well
stricken in years.  And the angel
answering said ... thou shalt be
dumb, and not be able to speak,
until the day that these things
shall be performed, because
thou believest not my words,
which shall be fulfilled in their
season."  (Luke 1:18-20)

## SEARCH #4
John and Jesus

**Mary and Joseph To Be Married**

"And in the sixth month the
angel Gabriel was sent from
God unto a city of Galilee,
named Nazareth, To a virgin
_ _ _ _ _ _ _ _
[promised to marry] to a man
whose name was Joseph, of the
house of David; and the virgin's
name was Mary." (Luke 1:26-27)

## SEARCH #5
John and Jesus

**Angel Gabriel Tells Mary**

**About Jesus**

"And the angel said unto her,
Fear not, Mary: for thou hast
found favour with God.  And
behold, thou shalt
_ _ _ _ _ _ _ _ in thy
womb, and bring forth a son,
and shalt call his name JESUS.
He shall be great, and shall be
called the Son of the Highest."
(Luke 1:30-32)

## SEARCH #6
John and Jesus

**Elisabeth and Mary Obey**

**Heavenly Father**

"And, behold, thy cousin
Elisabeth, she hath also
conceived a son in her old age:
and this is the sixth month with
her, who was called barren.
And Mary said, Behold the
handmaid of the Lord; be it
unto me according to
thy _ _ _ _ _.  And the angel
departed from her."
(Luke 1:36, 38)

**PATTERNS:** PONDER Cards #1-6

---

## PONDER #1
John and Jesus

### Elisabeth and Zacharias
### Want a Baby

Elisabeth and Zacharias were very old when they lived in Jersaulem.

What did they want more than anything else in the world?
(Luke 1:7)

A _ _ _ _ _

---

## PONDER #2
John and Jesus

### Angel Gabriel Tells Zacharias
### About John the Baptist

Zacharias was to have a son named John (the Baptist). What kind of man was Zacharias?

CIRCLE ANSWER(S):

☐ Young man
☐ Very old man
☐ Wicked man
☐ Priest who lived the commandments
(Luke 1:5-7)

---

## PONDER #3
John and Jesus

### Doubting Zacharias Is Punished

Zacharias was told by the Angel Gabriel he would have a son. He told the angel he didn't believe him. What did he say?
(Luke 1:18-20)

Choice #1  I am too old a man and my wife is stricken in years.

Choice #2  Who told you?

Check your choice(s):
#1 ☐ #2 ☐ None above ☐

---

## PONDER #4
John and Jesus

### Mary and Joseph To Be Married

Mary, who was to be the mother of Jesus, was promised to Joseph. What does "promised" mean?

CIRCLE ANSWER(S):
☐ Angry with Joseph
☐ In love with Joseph
☐ Married to Joseph
☐ Espoused (engaged to marry Joseph)
(Luke 1:26-27)

---

## PONDER #5
John and Jesus

### Angel Gabriel Tells Mary
### About Jesus

What did the Angel Gabriel tell Mary about herself and Jesus?
(Luke 1:30-31)

Mary had found
_ _ _ _ _ _ with God.

She would be the m_t_e_ of JESUS.

---

## PONDER #6
John and Jesus

### Elisabeth and Mary Obey
### Heavenly Father

How many months had Elisabeth been pregnant with baby John when her cousin Mary told her about baby Jesus?
(Luke 1:36)
_ _ _ months

What did Mary say that showed she wanted to obey the Lord and be the mother of baby Jesus?
"According to thy _ _ _ _ _."
(Luke 1:38)

# Scripture Show-and-Tell

### Angel Tells of Two Births:  John and Jesus, puppet show

♥     Copy and cut out cue cards that follow.     ♥  Copy, color, and cut out sack puppets #1-6 (patterns on pages 15-20).  Mount top of head to the bottom of a small sack, and mount the mouth under the flap (see below).

SEARCH, PONDER, and PLAY

**PRESENTATION PLAN:**
**Cards #1-6**

## Scripture Show-and-Tell
### An Angel Tells of Two Births

| SHOW:  Enter Puppets | SCENE: | | TELL:  Cue Cards #1-6 |
|---|---|---|---|
| Elisabeth and Zacharias | One | Elisabeth and Zacharias Want a Baby | #1 |
| Zacharias, Angel Gabriel, and Baby John | Two | Angel Tells Zacharias About Baby John | #2 |
| Mary, Angel Gabriel, and Baby Jesus | Three | Angel Tells Mary About Jesus | #3 |
| Mary and Joseph | Four | Mary and Joseph Were to Be Married | |
| Angel and Joseph | Five | Angel Tells Joseph About Baby Jesus | #4 |
| Mary and Elisabeth | Six | Elisabeth and Mary Were Cousins | |
| Elisabeth, Zacharias, and John | Seven | Baby John Was Born | #5 |
| Mary, Joseph, and Baby Jesus | Eight | Jesus Was Born | #6 |

♥ CUT outside line of both cards–DON'T cut center lines.  ♥ Fold between center line to CREATE A FOLDER to store cards #1-6.

CUT OUT cards #1-6 to rehearse Show-and-Tell presentation.

SEARCH, PONDER, and PLAY
Elisabeth and Zacharias Want a Baby

**Scene One: Show Elisabeth and Zacharias puppets and say:**

Scripture Show-and-Tell
**Cue Card #1**
**An Angel Tells of Two Births**

**NARRATOR:** Elisabeth was married to Zacharias. They lived in Jerusalem. They obeyed God's commandments. They were both very old, but they still prayed for a child.

**ELISABETH:** It would be so wonderful if we could have a baby. I love children. It would be so nice to have a little son or a daughter to love and take care of.

**ZACHARIAS:** It sure would. But, as you know, we are too old to have children. I have lost hope.

EXIT Elisabeth

SEARCH, PONDER, and PLAY
Angel Tells Zacharias About Baby John

**SCENE Two: Show Zacharias, Angel Gabriel puppets (shine flashlight in sack) and say:**

Scripture Show-and-Tell
**Cue Card #2**
**An Angel Tells of Two Births**

**NARRATOR:** Zacharias was a priest and worked in the temple. One day the Angel Gabriel appeared to him.

**GABRIEL:** Don't be afraid. Heavenly Father has sent me here to bless you and Elisabeth. God has answered your prayers. Elisabeth will have a baby. His name will be John. God has a work for John to do. He will hold the priesthood of God, and tell the people about Jesus Christ, the Son of God. John will be a righteous prophet.

**ZACHARIAS:** I do not believe you. Elisabeth is too old to have a baby.

**GABRIEL:** God sent me to tell you that this is true. Because you do not believe what God has said, you will not be able to speak until John is born.

**NARRATOR:** Zacharias came out of the temple and could not speak. Elisabeth now was going to have a baby. Baby John was the child they had always dreamed of.

EXIT Zacharias and Angel

SEARCH, PONDER, and PLAY
Angel Tells Mary About Jesus

Scene Three: Show Angel Gabriel (shine flashlight in sack) and Mary puppets and say:

**NARRATOR:** The Angel Gabriel came to Mary.
**GABRIEL:** Be not afraid. God loves you and wants to bless you more than any other woman, as you will have a special baby boy. His name will be Jesus. He will be the king of all righteous people.
**MARY:** But I do not have a husband.
**GABRIEL:** With God, nothing shall be impossible. Jesus will be the Son of God.
**MARY:** I will obey, and be the mother of Jesus.

Scripture Show-and-Tell
**Cue Card #3**
An Angel Tells of Two Births

EXIT Mary and Gabriel

---

SEARCH, PONDER, and PLAY
Mary and Joseph Were to Be Married
Angel Tells Joseph About Baby Jesus

Scene Four: Show Mary & Joseph puppets and say:

**NARRATOR:** Mary and Joseph lived in Nazareth. They were righteous. They always tried to choose the right. Mary and Joseph loved each other and wanted to be married.

EXIT Mary

Scene Five: Show Angel & Joseph puppets and say:

**NARRATOR:** The angel appeared to Joseph in a dream.
**ANGEL:** Mary's baby is the Son of God. Take Mary as your wife and name the baby Jesus. Jesus will be the Savior of the world.
**JOSEPH:** I will obey.

Scripture Show-and-Tell
**Cue Card #4**
An Angel Tells of Two Births

EXIT Angel and Joseph

SEARCH, PONDER, and PLAY
Elisabeth and Mary Were Cousins Baby John was Born

**Scene Six : Show Mary, Elisabeth, Baby John, and Baby Jesus puppets and say:**

Scripture Show-and-Tell
## Cue Card #5
**An Angel Tells of Two Births**

NARRATOR: Mary visited her cousin Elisabeth. They were to have special children: Jesus Christ and John the Baptist. They were blessed more than any other women. Because Elisabeth and Mary were cousins, the babies John and Jesus would also be cousins.

EXIT
Mary,
Elisabeth,
Baby John,
and Jesus

**Scene Seven:  Show Elisabeth, Zacharias, and Baby John puppets and say:**

NARRATOR: Elisabeth's son John was born. Friends gathered around. Everyone was so happy! Friends thought Elisabeth should name the baby Zacharias, after the father. Elisabeth said "No." They asked Zacharias what to name the baby. He could not speak, so he wrote the name JOHN. Then Zacharias was able to speak. He was filled with the Holy Ghost and thanked God for baby John. Zacharias told the people that Jesus would be born soon.

EXIT
Elisabeth,
Zacharias,
and
Baby John

---

SEARCH, PONDER and PLAY
Jesus Was Born

**Scene Eight:  Show Mary, Joseph, and Baby Jesus and say:**

Scripture Show-and-Tell
## Cue Card #6
**An Angel Tells of Two Births**

NARRATOR:  Joseph and Mary had to go to Bethlehem to pay their taxes.  Mary was very tired, as she would have the baby soon.  Many people were in Bethlehem, and there were no rooms left.
JOSEPH:  I found a place where you can have the baby.  It is a stable, a place for animals, but the baby will be warm.
Mary:  Thank you, Joseph.  I am so tired.
NARRATOR:  Mary had the baby Jesus, and a star shone bright over the manger to direct the shepherds and wise men to the humble stable.  They came, and saw the baby Jesus wrapped in swaddling clothes, lying in a manger.  Mary and Joseph were so happy that they could help take care of Jesus, the Savior of us all.
## THE END

SEARCH, PONDER, and PLAY

**Game Baby Spoons and Baby News Match**

**GAME**
**An Angel Tells of Two Birth**

**OBJECTIVE:** Match cards to get acquainted with Elizabeth, Zacharias, Baby John, Mary, Joseph, and Baby Jesus. Make a match and grab for John and Jesus baby spoons for keeps!

**YOU'LL NEED:**
Copy of two double-sided baby spoons on page 5 and a set of match cards (copy pattern twice) on page 21, on light blue cardstock paper, for each guest.

**TO MAKE GAME AND PRIZES:**
1. Cut out double-sided spoons and match cards, and glue spoons back-to-back.
2. Create "We Love Babies" medallion (pages 13, and 22) to wear while playing this game.

**HOW TO PLAY:**
1. <u>Set Up</u>: Players sit in a circle. Shuffle and give four cards to each player. Place remaining cards in center, with spoons surrounding cards (two spoons per player).
2. <u>First Player</u> looks at his cards for a match. Player lays down all matching cards and then discards one card to the player on his left.
3. <u>Next</u> player plays.
4. <u>Start With Four Cards</u>: If a player starts out with less than four cards in his hand, he draws from the center pile until he has four cards.
5. <u>SPOON GRAB</u>: As soon as a player lays down four matched sets, he can say, "BABY NEWS!" and grab a spoon. Player keeps the spoon as a prize. Go on to next player.

> **BE AN ANGEL AND FOLLOW THIS RULE:** When players lay down a match, they must lay it face up so other players can anticipate a spoon grab. Once player grabs a spoon, they return matched sets to the center pile and start over.

6. <u>Beat 'em</u>: When a player makes a match and gets ready to say "**BABY NEWS!**", the other players can beat them to it by saying "**YOU SNOOZE.**" Then that player has to return his matched cards to the center pile and start over. He doesn't get a spoon.
7. <u>To Win</u>: Play until all spoons are gone. Player with the most spoons says:

**"I WON BABY NEWS! YOU SNOOZE!"**
Prizes: Players divide spoons.

SEARCH, PONDER, and PLAY

### "We Love Babies" medallion

**OBJECTIVE:**  Share the excitement that Zacharias, Elizabeth, Mary, and Joseph felt when the babies arrived.  Wear medallion while playing the Baby Spoons and Baby News Match game (see page 12).

**YOU'LL NEED:**
Copy of medallion pattern on page 22 on light blue cardstock paper for each guest, crayons or markers, scissors, paper punch, and yarn or ribbon

### John and Jesus baby spoons

**OBJECTIVE:** Collect baby spoons to remember two important babies.

### FAVORS or PRIZES
**An Angel Tells of Two Births**

**To Make Medallion:**
1. Color and cut out medallion.
2. Punch a hole at the top.
3. Tie yarn or ribbon to fit around guest's neck.

**COLLECT BABY SPOONS:** Play the Baby Spoons and Baby News Match game to collect baby spoons (page 5).  After, insert baby spoon in Baby Newsletter by cutting slits with a razor blade (page 3).

---

SEARCH, PONDER and PLAY

### BABY LOVE MILK
(milk with "Baby Love Milk" label on cup)

**YOU'LL NEED:**  Copy of "Baby Love Milk" label on page 23 on light blue lightweight paper, milk, tape, and an 8-ounce paper cup for each guest, scissors, and crayons

**TO MAKE CUP & SERVE MILK:**
1. Color and cut out label.
2. Tape label to an 8-ounce cup.
3. Fill with cold milk and serve.

**ACTIVITY:**  Read the scripture above and be happy for Mary and Elisabeth, who knew that they would each have a special child.  As you drink your milk, say, "We love babies, and we love milk!"

### Thought Treat
**An Angel Tells of Two Births**
Luke 1:39-42

SEARCH, PONDER, and PLAY

## ANGEL FOOD CAKE
(cake decorated with coconut and sign)

**YOU'LL NEED:** Copy of "Angel Tells of Two Births" sign below on light blue cardstock paper, frosting, whipped cream or non-dairy topping (optional), coconut (optional), and two toothpicks

**TO MAKE & DECORATE CAKE:**
1. Bake and frost an angel food cake.
OPTION: Cut into individual slices and place a sign on top of each piece.
2. Color and cut out sign(s).
3. Pierce each side of sign with a toothpick and stick on top of cake.

**ANGEL FROSTING:** Mix frosting with 1/3 part non-dairy whipped topping.
Option: Add blue food coloring to make cake light blue. Frost cake. Sprinkle coconut on top and sides of cake.

**ACTIVITY:** Read the scriptures above and say, "Gabriel was an angel to come and tell us the good news about baby John and Jesus."

**PATTERN:**  Elisabeth sack puppet for Scripture Show-and-Tell   ♥ Copy on flesh-colored cardstock paper.

**PATTERN:** Zacharias sack puppet for Scripture Show-and-Tell  ♥ Copy on flesh-colored cardstock paper.

**PATTERN:**  Angel Gabriel sack puppet for Show-and-Tell ♥ Copy on flesh-colored cardstock paper.  Shine flashlight through sack.

**PATTERN:** Baby John & Jesus sack puppets for Scripture Show-and-Tell ♥ Copy on flesh-colored cardstock paper.

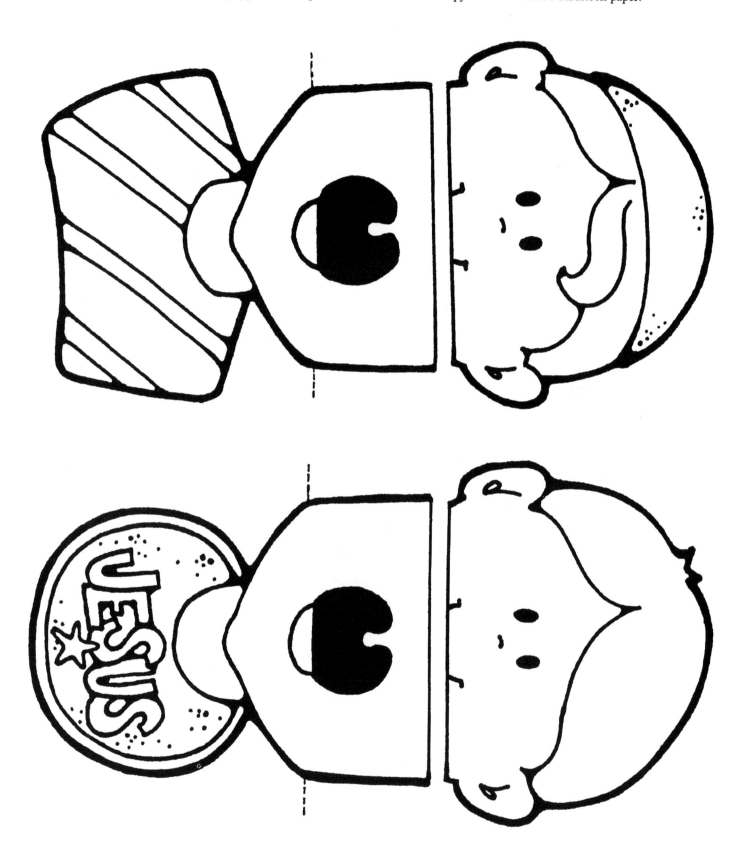

**PATTERN:**  Mary sack puppet for Scripture Show-and-Tell   ♥ Copy on flesh-colored cardstock paper.

**PATTERN:**  Joseph sack puppet for Scripture Show-and-Tell  ♥ Copy on flesh-colored cardstock paper.

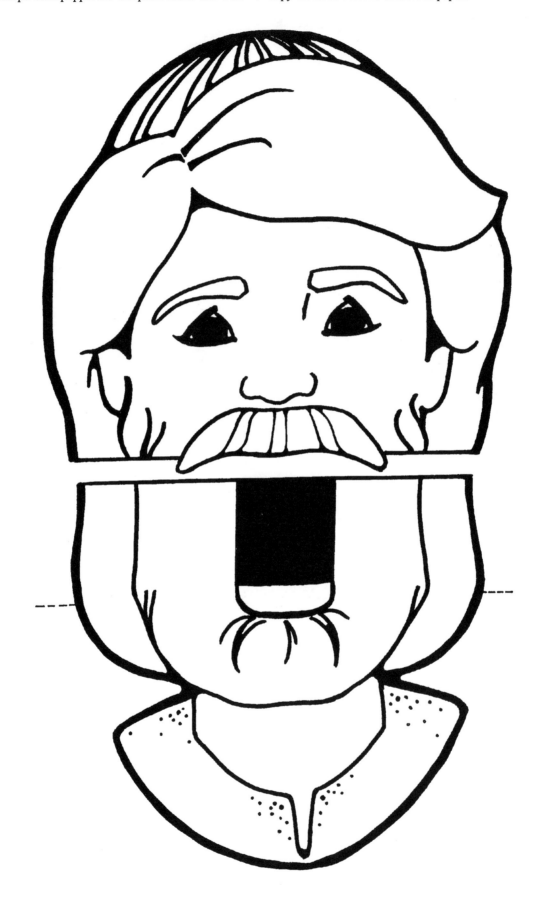

**PATTERN:** Baby News Match game cards (two sets for each guest)  ♥ Copy on light blue cardstock paper.

**PATTERN:** We Love Babies medallion favor ♥ Copy on light blue cardstock paper.

**PATTERN:**  Baby Love Milk label for Thought Treat   ♥ Copy on light blue cardstock paper.

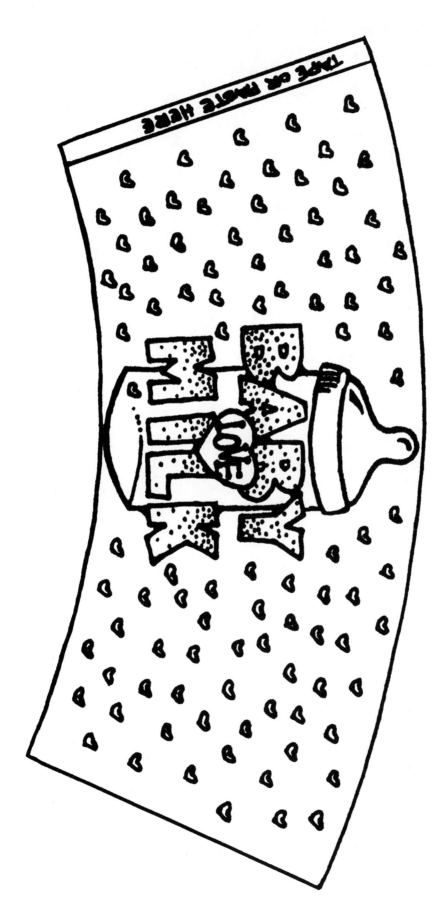

**PATTERN:**  BONUS MOTIVATORS "You're an Angel" certificate and glue-on stickers for completing the "John and Jesus" Search and Ponder cards ♥ Copy one for each guest.

## You're an Angel for Learning the Stories of Jesus

Certificate Awarded

To: _____

on _____
(date you completed the "Jesus and John"
Search and Ponder cards)

## CONGRATULATIONS!

## You're an Angel for Learning the Stories of Jesus

Certificate Awarded

To: _____

on _____
(date you completed the "Jesus and John"
Search and Ponder cards)

## CONGRATULATIONS!

PLACE ACTIVITIES IN FILE FOLDER: Cut out and mount label and checklist on folder.

→
↓

New Testament

# Fishers of Men:
## Jesus Chose 12 Apostles

Swim on over for "Fishers of Men" SCRIPTURE PARTY!

To: _____
Date: _____ Time: _____
Place: _____
Bring invitation to the party!

## SCRIPTURE ACTIVITY CHECKLIST
Fishers of Men: Jesus Chose 12 Apostles

PAGES:

Jesus chose 12 apostles to be fishers of men. They *"Straightway left their nets, and followed him."* (Matthew 4:17-20). We too can be fishers of men. We can be an example to others, share the gospel with them, and bear our testimony.

Let's learn how to be a disciple of Jesus Christ

Let's remember the comforter he left. The Holy Ghost can be an anchor in our lives. If we listen and obey his still small voice, he will guide us out of dangerous waters. He will be our constant companion until Jesus returns.

**DO AHEAD:**
☐ Copy patterns . . . . 36-50
☐ Create Invitation or Favor: Fishers of Men boat with fish pond tickets . . . . 26
☐ Gather supplies*

PAGES:

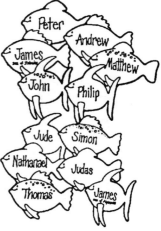

Peter, Andrew, James, Matthew, John, Philip, Jude, Simon, Nathanael, Judas, Thomas, James

## S E A R C H  and  P O N D E R :

☐ SEARCH & PONDER cards . . . . . . . . . . . . . . . . . . . . . . 27-28
☐ SCRIPTURE SHOW-AND-TELL: Rehearse cue cards for presentation: Fishers of Men: Jesus Chose 12 Apostles poster . . . . 29-32

## P L A Y :  SUPER SCRIPTURE ACTIVITY Choices

☐ SCRIPTURE SHOW-AND-TELL presentation
☐ ACTIVITY: GO FISH: Disciple Decisions . . . . . . . . . . . . . . . . . . 33
☐ SONGS:
  ○ "I Feel My Savior's Love," page 74**
  ○ "Love One Another," page 136**
  ○ "Jesus Is Our Loving Friend," page 58**
  ○ "I'm Trying to Be Like Jesus," page 78**
☐ FAVORS and PRIZES: . . . . . . . . . . . . . . . . . 34
  ○ Fish-ionary Tie
  ○ Fishers of Men goodie sack
☐ THOUGHT TREATS: . . . . . . . . . . . . . . . . . . . 35
  ○ Fish Sticks served in fish sack
  ○ Jiggly Jelly Fish Pond
☐ BONUS MOTIVATORS: . . . . . . . . . . . . . . 49-50

**\*SUPPLIES:**
Pattern copies, scissors, crayons or markers, zip-close plastic sandwich bags, string, paper punch, fish candy or crackers, and Thought Treats

I am a disciple of Jesus Christ.

SUPPLEMENTAL READING--New Testament Stories**: Jesus Chooses His Apostles, Jesus Commands the Wind and the Waves, Jesus Feeds 5,000 People, Jesus Walks on the Water, Jesus Blesses the Children, The Savior Goes to Jerusalem, and The First Sacrament

**Children's Songbook and New Testament Stories are published by The Church of Jesus Christ of Latter-day Saints, Salt Lake City, Utah.

Jesus and the Apostles ate...

FISH, FISH, FISH!

**PATTERN:** Fishing boat invitation/favor with tickets for fish pond ♥ Copy patterns on colored cardstock paper.

**FAVOR:**
Copy and cut out "Fishers of Men" boat on page 36 and tickets #1 and #2 (right). Tape a zip-close plastic bag on the front of each boat with double-stick tape, and enclose tickets. Tickets will be used for the GO FISH activity detailed on page 33.

**INVITATION:**
If having a SUPER SCRIPTURE ACTIVITY, copy the fish invitation below. Enclose in "Fishers of Men" boat bag with tickets (detailed above). Guests are instructed to bring boat and tickets to the to GO FISH activity.

## Scripture SEARCH and PONDER:

♥ Copy two sets of SEARCH and PONDER cards below on colored cardstock paper.  ♥ Cut out cards.
- ◻ <u>Use Set #1</u> for Daily Devotionals.
- ◻ OPTION: Make a second set of cards to play The New Testament Game--Spotlighting the Life of Jesus. (This game is found on pages 59-60 of SUPER SCRIPTURE ACTIVITIES--NEW TESTAMENT, by Mary H. Ross and Jennette Guymon. Copy each set of cards a different color to identify quickly, i.e. copy this set light green.)

---

### SEARCH #1
Fishers of Men

**Jesus Prepared and Began**

**His Mission**

Heavenly Father was happy that Jesus was baptized.  He said, "This is my beloved Son, in whom I am _ _ _ _ _ pleased." (Matthew 3:17)
Jesus said no to temptation. "Jesus ... _ _ _ _ _ _ _ forty days and forty nights ... Then saith unto him, Get thee hence, Satan."
(Matthew 4:1-2, 10)
"Jesus began to preach, and to say, Repent: for the kingdom of _ _ _ _ _ _ _ is at hand."
(Matthew 4:17)

---

### SEARCH #2
Fishers of Men

**Jesus Chose 12 Apostles:**

**Fishers of Men**

"And he saith unto them,

_ _ _ _ _ _ me, and I will make you fishers of men.  And they straightway left their _ _ _ _ , and followed him."
(Matthew 4:19-20)

---

### SEARCH #3
Fishers of Men

**The Apostles Were**

**Good Examples**

"He that hath my commandments, and _ _ _ _ _ _ _ _ them, he it is that loveth me: and he that loveth me shall be loved of my Father, and I will love him, and will manifest [show] myself to him."  (John 14:21)

---

### SEARCH #4
Fishers of Men

**The Apostles Were**

**Teachers of Men**

"When thou art

_ _ _ _ _ _ _ _ _ _ , strengthen thy brethren."
(Luke 22:32)
"Go ye therefore, and teach all nations,

_ _ _ _ _ _ _ _ them in the name of the Father, and of the Son, and of the Holy Ghost:  Teaching them to observe all things whatsoever I have commanded you: and, lo, I am with you alway, even unto the end of the world."
(Matthew 28:19-20)

---

### SEARCH #5
Fishers of Men

**The Apostles Were**

**Special Witnesses of Jesus**

"And ye also shall _ _ _ _ _ witness, because ye have been with me from the beginning."
(John 15:27)

"And this is life eternal, that they might _ _ _ _ _ thee the only true God, and Jesus Christ, whom thou hast sent."
(John 17:3)

---

### SEARCH #6
Fishers of Men

**Jesus Sent the Holy Ghost:**

**Our Anchor**

"Yet a little while, and the world seeth me no more; but ye see me:  because I live, ye shall _ _ _ _ _ live also."
(John 14:19)

"The Comforter, which is the Holy Ghost, ... shall _ _ _ _ _ _ you all things, and bring all things to your remembrance." (John 14:26)

The comforter is an anchor, to keep us out of dangerous waters.

**PATTERNS:** PONDER Cards #1-6

---

## PONDER #1
Fishers of Men

### Jesus Prepared and Began
### His Mission

What did Jesus do in the wilderness to learn of Heavenly Father's plan? (Matthew 4:2)
_ _ _ _ _ _ forty days and forty nights

What did Jesus tell the people to do, to be a part of Heavenly Father's kingdom?
(Matthew 4:17)

R _ _ _ _ t

---

## PONDER #2
Fishers of Men

### Jesus Chose 12 Apostles:
### Fishers of Men

How did Jesus first choose his apostles by the sea?
(Matthew 4:19)
He ask them to follow him, that he would make them
_ _ _ _ _ _ _ of men.

What did the apostles do when Jesus asked them to go with him? (Matthew 4:20)

Left their nets
and _ _ _ _ _ _ _ _ him

---

## PONDER #3
Fishers of Men

### The Apostles Were
### Good Examples

How do you show Heavenly Father and Jesus that you love them?

Keep _ _ _ _ _ _ _ -
_ _ _ _ _ _ (one word)

---

## PONDER #4
Fishers of Men

### The Apostles Were
### Teachers of Men

What do you do when you gain a testimony (are converted)?
(Luke 22:32)

Strengthen your

_ _ _ _ _ _ _ _

How many nations should you teach? (Matthew 28:19)

_ _ _

---

## PONDER #5
Fishers of Men

### The Apostles Were
### Special Witnesses of Jesus

How long had the apostles been with Jesus? (John 15:27)
"From the
_ _ _ _ _ _ _ _ _ " of his mission to the end of his mission

What was the mission of Jesus and the apostles? (John 17:3)
To "know thee the only true God, and _ _ _ _ _ _
_ _ _ _ _ _ whom thou hast sent."

---

## PONDER #6
Fishers of Men

### The Apostles Witness Jesus:
### Their Mission

What is the comforter's name who takes the place of Jesus when he is gone from the earth?
(John 14:26)

_ _ _ _  _ _ _ _ _

This comforter will testify to you that Jesus and Heavenly Father live.
What is he known as?
(John 15:26)
The _ _ _ _ _ _ of truth

# Scripture Show-and-Tell

## Fishers of Men: Jesus Chose 12 Apostles poster

♥ Copy and cut out cue cards that follow. ♥ Copy, color water waves, boat, apostle fish, and anchor (patterns on pages 37-45). OPTION: Draw a fish net on light blue poster paper and copy water waves on light blue paper to place on top. All patterns can be posted on a board or poster paper (see layout below).

SEARCH, PONDER, and PLAY

**PRESENTATION PLAN:
Cards #1-6**

### Scripture Show-and-Tell
#### Fishers of Men

**SHOW: boat and water wordstrips, fish, and anchor**          **TELL: Cue Cards #1-6**

Fishers of Men boat wordstrip and
Jesus Chose 12 Apostles water wordstrip

|  |  |
|---|---|
|  | Jesus Prepared and Began His Mission . . . . . . . . . . Card #1 |
| APOSTLE fish | Jesus Chose 12 Apostles: Fishers of Men . . . . . . . Card #2 |
| EXAMPLE fish | The Apostles Were Good Examples . . . . . . . . . . . Card #3 |
| TEACHER fish | The Apostles Were Teachers of Men . . . . . . . . . . Card #4 |
| SPECIAL WITNESS fish | The Apostles Were Special Witnesses of Jesus . . . . Card #5 |
| COMFORTER anchor | Jesus Sent the Holy Ghost: Our Anchor . . . . . . . . Card #6 |

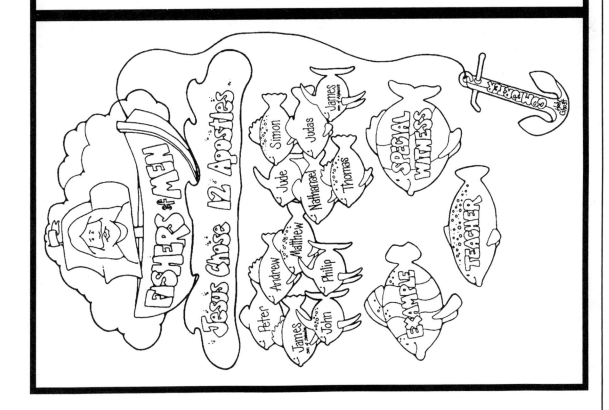

CUT OUT cards #1-6 to rehearse Show-and-Tell presentation.

SEARCH, PONDER, and PLAY
Jesus Prepared and Began His Mission

**Place Fishers of Men boat and Jesus Chose 12 Apostles water wordstrips on the board and say:**

Scripture Show-and-Tell
# Cue Card #1
**Fishers of Men**

Jesus and his apostles were FISHERS OF MEN.  Jesus prepared for his mission and then he chose 12 apostles.  They would help him heal the sick, and teach men to repent and be baptized, so they could live with Heavenly Father.  First, Jesus prepared for his mission:

♥ Jesus Was Baptized in the River Jordan, and Heavenly Father said, *"This is my beloved Son, in whom I am well pleased."* (Matthew 3:17)

♥ Jesus Fasted and Prayed forty days and nights in the wilderness.  Satan tempted Jesus, but he said "no."  He was there to learn from Heavenly Father.

♥ Jesus Began His Mission, saying to the people:  *"Repent: for the kingdom of heaven is at hand."* (Matthew 4:17)

SEARCH, PONDER, and PLAY
Jesus Chose 12 Apostles:  Fishers of Men

**Place 12 APOSTLES fish to left and right of boat and say:**

Scripture Show-and-Tell
# Cue Card #2
**Fishers of Men**

While walking by the sea of Galilee, Jesus saw two brethren, Simon called Peter, and Andrew his brother, casting a net into the sea, for they were fishermen.  *"And he saith unto them, Follow me, and I will make you fishers of men.  And they straightway left their nets, and followed him."* (Matthew 4:19-20)

The 12 apostles he chose were to be fishers of men, to convert the people to the gospel of Jesus Christ.  He ordained them to the priesthood.

They were:  Peter, James (son of Zebedee), John, Andrew, Matthew, Philip, Jude, Nathanael, Thomas, Simon, Judas, and James (son of Alphaeus).

SEARCH, PONDER, and PLAY
The Apostles Were Good Examples

Place EXAMPLE fish on board and say:

Scripture Show-and-Tell
**Cue Card #3**
Fishers of Men

The apostles were good examples for all to follow. They tried to be like Jesus.

They followed in his footsteps and tried to keep the commandments. They knew that obeying the commandments would bring them closer to Jesus and to Heavenly Father.

Jesus said:   "*He that hath my commandments, and keepeth them, he it is that loveth me: and he that loveth me shall be loved of my Father, and I will love him, and will manifest [show] myself to him.*" (John 14:21)

SEARCH, PONDER, and PLAY
The Apostles Were Teachers of Men

Place TEACHER fish on board and say:

Scripture Show-and-Tell
**Cue Card #4**
Fishers of Men

Thousands of people followed Jesus and the apostles from Galilee, Jerusalem, Judea, and beyond Jordan. They heard of his teachings and miracles.

Jesus wanted the apostles to teach others about the gospel of Jesus Christ. He said to Simon Peter, "*I have prayed for thee, that thy faith fail not: and when thou art converted, strengthen thy brethren.*" (Luke 22:32)

He said:  "*Go ye therefore, and teach all nations, baptizing them in the name of the Father, and of the Son, and of the Holy Ghost: Teaching them to observe all things whatsoever I have commanded you: and, lo, I am with you alway, even unto the end of the world.*" (Matthew 28:19-20)

The apostles were not alone in their missionary assignments. Jesus guided them while he was on the earth, and sent a comforter when he left.

SEARCH, PONDER, and PLAY
The Apostles Were Special Witnesses of Jesus

**Place SPECIAL WITNESS fish on board and say:**

Scripture Show-and-Tell
## Cue Card #5
**Fishers of Men**

The apostles were special witnesses of Jesus.  They shared their testimony with others about his life and the truths he taught.

The first four books of the New Testament were written by four witnesses, the apostles Matthew, Mark, Luke, and John.  They told his story, from his birth to his death and resurrection.  They told how they were called by him to be fishers of men.  They were proud to be his friends.

They told of the miracles he performed--when he calmed the seas, walked on water, and fed the 5,000 with only five loaves of bread and two fish.  How did he do these things?  He had the priesthood, the power of God.  He healed the sick, and raised others from the dead.

---

SEARCH, PONDER, and PLAY
Jesus Sent the Holy Ghost:  Our Anchor

**Place COMFORTER anchor on board and say:**

Scripture Show-and-Tell
## Cue Card #6
**Fishers of Men**

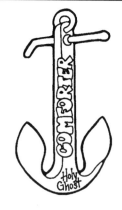

When it came time for him to be crucified, Jesus knew what would happen. He told the apostles:  *"Yet a little while, and the world seeth me no more; but ye see me:  because I live, ye shall live also."* (John 14:19)

He knew the apostles loved him, and he loved the apostles.  Because they loved him, they were sad that he was leaving.

He told them he would send a special spirit to guide them.  Jesus said:  *"The Comforter, which is the Holy Ghost, ... shall teach you all things, and bring all things to your remembrance."* (John 14:26)

This comforter is an anchor in our lives.  A boat needs an anchor to keep it from moving into dangerous waters.  If we listen to the still, small voice, it will keep us from danger by teaching us truths and giving us guidance.

SEARCH, PONDER, and PLAY

### ACTIVITY: GO FISH: Disciple Decisions
Prizes: Fish-ionary tie and Fishers of Men goodie sack

## ACTIVITY
**Fishers of Men**

**YOU'LL NEED:** Copies of patterns and supplies:
- ♦ Pond Decoration: Show-and-Tell patterns on pages 37-45
- ♦ GO FISH tickets #1 and #2 for each guest (see page 26)
- ♦ Fish pond prizes (see pages 46-47): Fish-ionary tie and Fishers of Men goodie sack (filled with fish candy or crackers)
- ♦ Fishing pole (string, stick, and paper clip for fish hook)
- ♦ Supplies: Scissors, crayons or markers and string

### HOW TO MAKE:
- ♦ FISH POND:
1. Color Fishers of Men wordstrip and apostle fish.
2. Drape a sheet or large towel over the backs of two chairs.
- ♦ FISHING POLE:
1. Tie a string on stick, and paper clip for hook.
2. Bend hook to attach prizes.
- ♦ FISH POND PRIZES: See pages 34 to make Fish-ionary Tie and Fishers of Men goodie sack (using string).
- ♦ FISH POND TICKETS: You'll need a set of tickets #1 and #2 for each guest (see page 26). If sending an invitation, enclose tickets in invitation for guest to bring.
FUN OPTION: Guests collect prizes to take home in boat invitation/favor plastic bag.

PRIZES*

**GO FISH!** Guests line up in front of fish pond with ticket #1 and ticket #2 in hand. Tell guests the following:

Jesus chose 12 apostles to help him on his mission. They were: Peter, James, John, Andrew, Matthew, Philip, Jude, Nathanael, Thomas, Simon, Judas, and James. (Point to fish on fish pond as you say their names).

Jesus called them, saying, "*Follow me, and I will make you fishers of men. And they straightway left their nets, and followed him.*" (Matthew 4:17-20)
We too can be fishers of men. Let's GO FISH!

### HOW TO FISH:
**HOOK TICKET #1** on line and throw it over pond saying, "I want to be a disciple of Jesus." When an imaginary fish (person on other side of fish pond) yanks on your line, pull it over to collect your prize. Wait until others guests have fished, then:
**HOOK TICKET #2** on line and throw it over pond, saying: "I want to be a fisher of men." When a fish yanks on your line, pull it over to collect your prize.

*PRIZES to Match Tickets: Ticket #1 Fish-ionary tie, Ticket #2 Fishers of Men goodie sack

SEARCH, PONDER, and PLAY

### FISH-IONARY TIE:
(paper tie to wear around neck)

FAVOR or PRIZE

Fishers of Men

**OBJECTIVE:**
Tell how one can be a missionary or disciple of Jesus
Christ.  Guests can receive this during
GO FISH activity (see page 33 for details).

**YOU'LL NEED:**
Copy of Fish-ionary tie pattern on page 46 for each
guest, scissors, crayons or markers, paper punch, and
string.

**TO MAKE TIE:**
Color and cut out tie, punch holes at the top, and tie
string to wear around neck.

---

SEARCH, PONDER, and PLAY

### FISHERS OF MEN goodie sack:
(sack with string attached, filled with
fish-shaped candy or crackers)

FAVOR or PRIZE

Fishers of Men

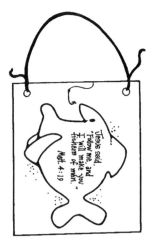

**OBJECTIVE:**   Tell how Jesus chose his first disciples,
telling them they could be fishers of men.  Tell how
the apostles followed Jesus.  Guests can receive this
during GO FISH activity on page 33.

**YOU'LL NEED:**   Copy goodie sack pattern on
page 47 on colored cardstock paper, scissors, crayons
or markers, paper punch, string, and fish-shaped candy
or crackers for each guest.

**TO MAKE GOODIE SACK:**
Color and cut out sack, fold tabs and glue together,
punch holes and tie a string at top.
Fill with candy fish or fish-shaped crackers.

SEARCH, PONDER, and PLAY

### FISH STICKS: (serve in a fish sack)

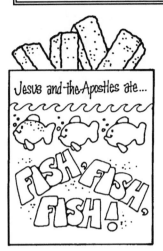

**Thought Treat**
**Fishers of Men**
Matthew 4:17-20

**You'll Need:** Copy of fish sticks sack on page 48 on colored cardstock paper, foil or waxed paper, ready-to-heat and serve fish sticks, and fish tartar sauce for each guest.

**To Make:**
Fish Stick Sack: Cut out fish sack, fold tabs and glue together.
Fish Sticks: Heat fish sticks (4 or 5 per guest), wrap the bottom half of them in foil or waxed paper, and serve in fish sticks sack.

**ACTIVITY:** Think of ways Jesus and his apostles cooked and served fish.

---

SEARCH, PONDER, and PLAY

### JIGGLY JELLY FISH POND:
(gelatin pond with fish afloat)

**Thought Treat**
**Fishers of Men**
Matthew 4:17-20

**You'll Need:**
TO MAKE POND: Two 6-ounce packages of blue or green gelatin dessert.
TO MAKE FISH: Two different colors, 6 ounces each, of yellow, red, or orange gelatin dessert.

**To Make:**
FISH POND: Make firm gelatin recipe, which requires two 6-ounce packages of blue or green gelatin dessert and water (read package). Pour hot gelatin into a 13 x 9-inch pan. Chill three hours or until firm.
JIGGLY JELLY FISH: Make firm gelatin recipe above, dividing water portion in half for each 6-ounce package to make firm fish of different colors. Pour hot gelatin into two individual cake or pie pans to set (refrigerate) 2 hours or until firm. Run warm water over bottom on pan and release gelatin onto waxed paper. Cut into fish shapes with a dull knife. Place fish on top of fish pond to serve. **ACTIVITY:** Read scripture above and GO FISH! Eat the gelatin fish pond with these sounds: "Slurp Slurp, Swish Swish." Enjoy your fish!

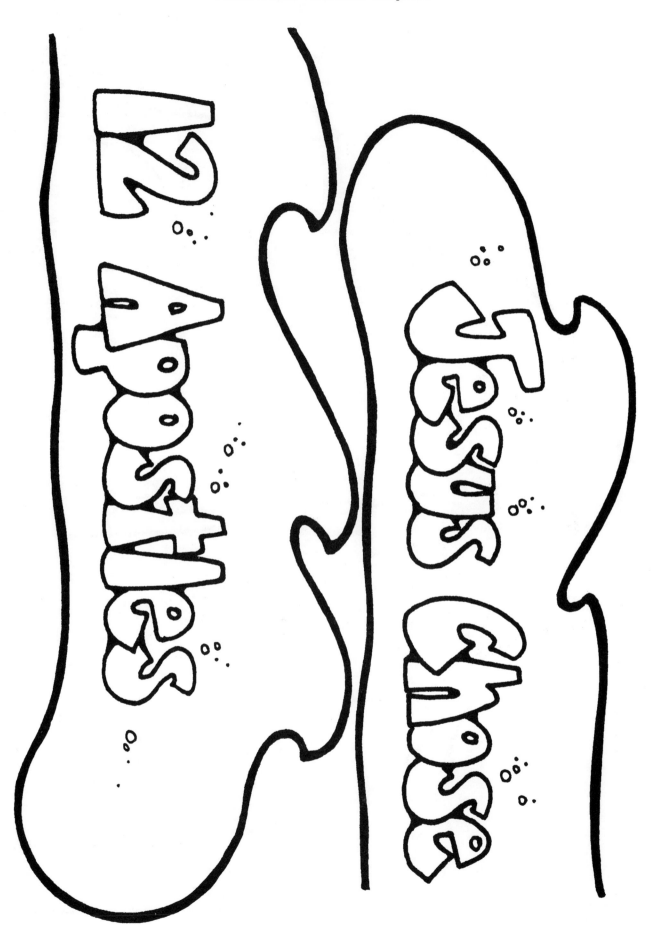

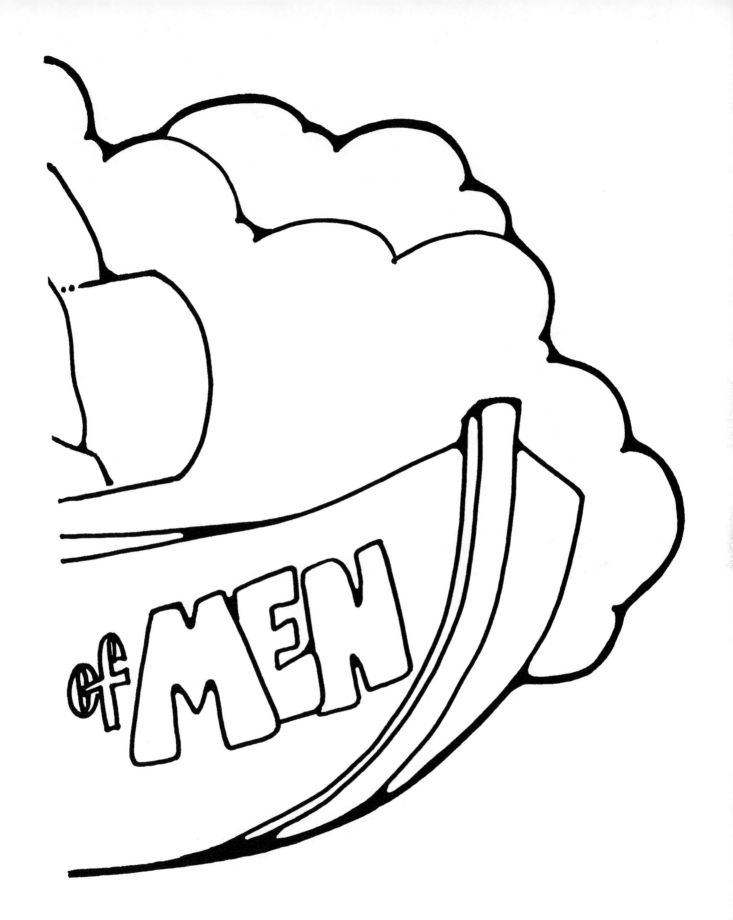

**PATTERN:**  APOSTLE fish for Scripture Show-and-Tell  ♥ Copy on cardstock paper.

**PATTERN:** APOSTLE fish for Scripture Show-and-Tell ♥ Copy on cardstock paper.

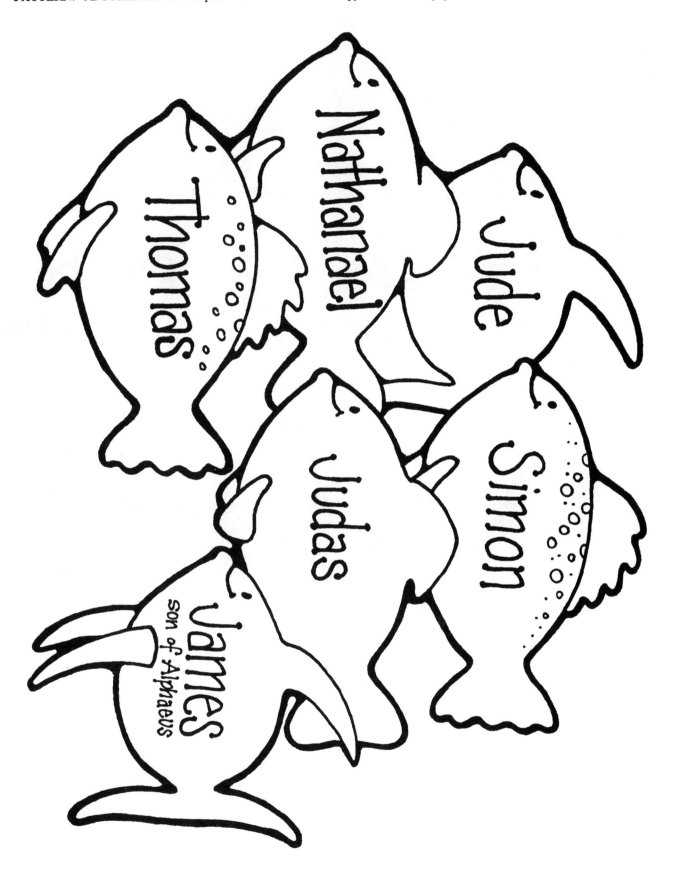

**PATTERN:** EXAMPLE fish for Scripture Show-and-Tell ♥ Copy on cardstock paper.

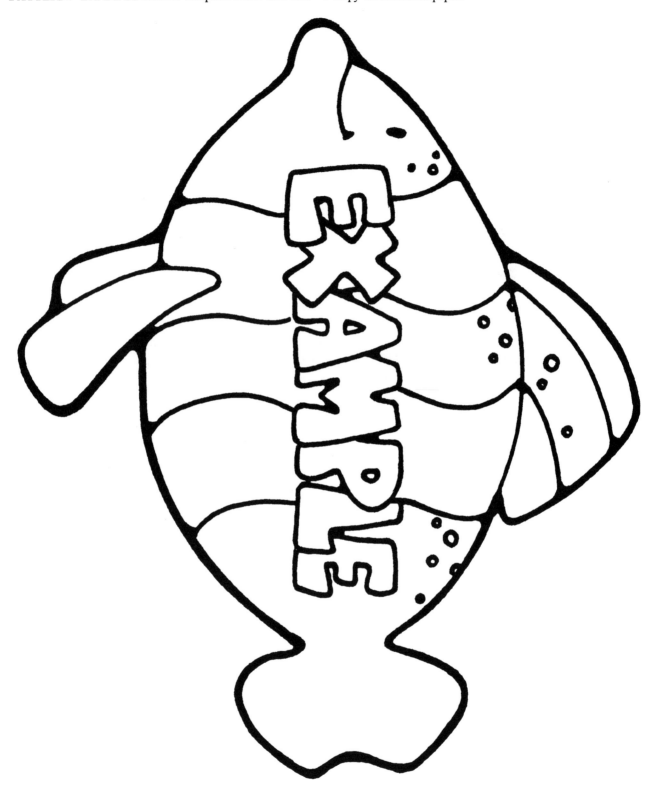

**PATTERN:** TEACHER fish for Scripture Show-and-Tell ♥ Copy on cardstock paper.

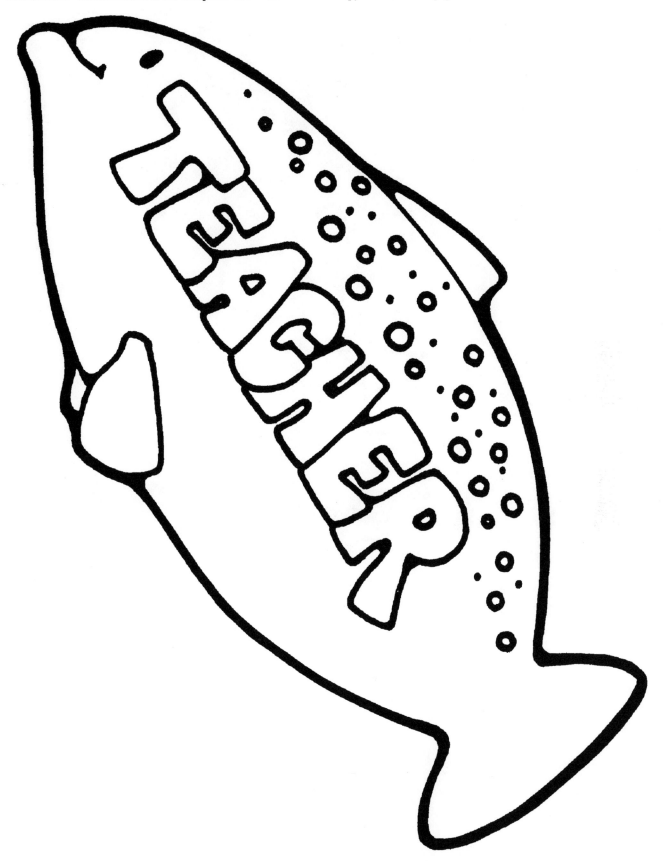

**PATTERN:** SPECIAL WITNESS fish for Scripture Show-and-Tell  ♥ Copy on cardstock paper.

**PATTERN:** COMFORTER (Holy Ghost) anchor for Scripture Show-and-Tell ♥ Copy on cardstock paper.

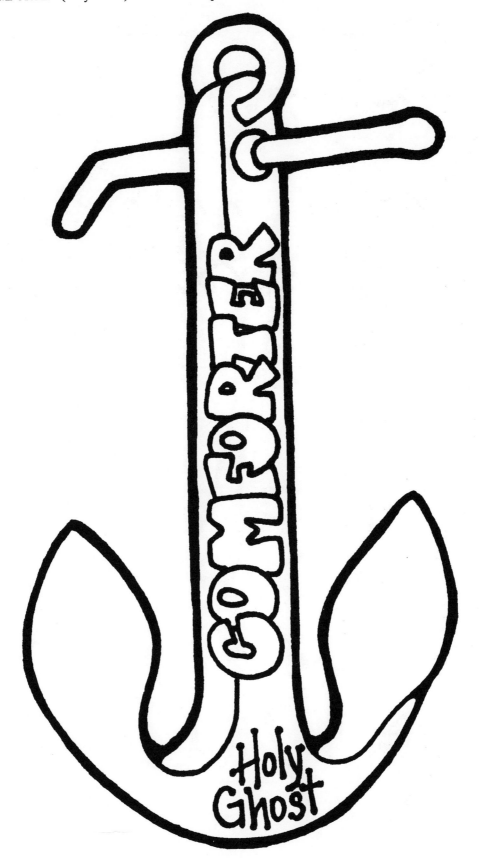

**PATTERN:** Fish-ionary fish tie favor or prize ♥ Copy on cardstock paper.

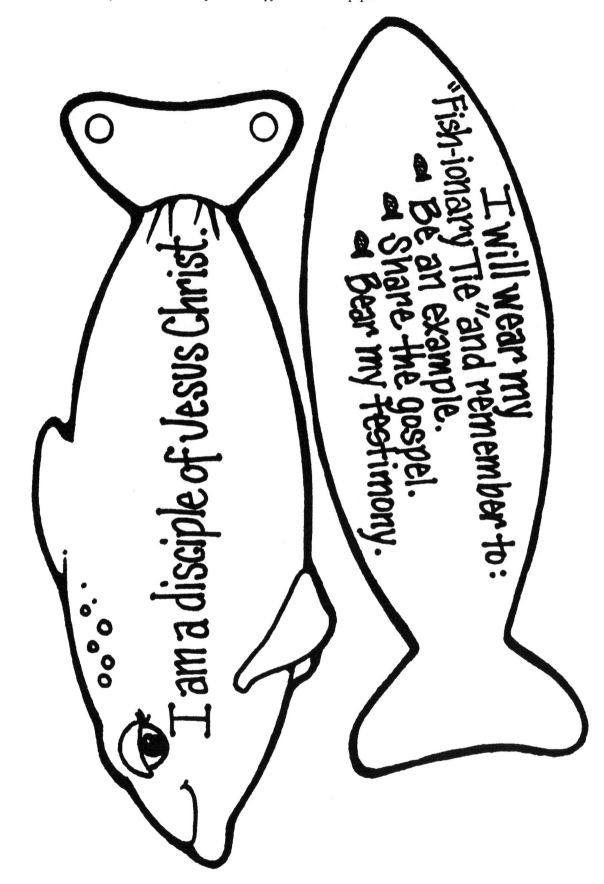

I am a disciple of Jesus Christ.

"Fish-ionary Tie" and remember to:
🐟 Be an example.
🐟 Share the gospel.
🐟 Bear my testimony.

I will wear my

**PATTERN:** Fishers of Men goodie sack favor or prize ♥ Copy on cardstock paper.

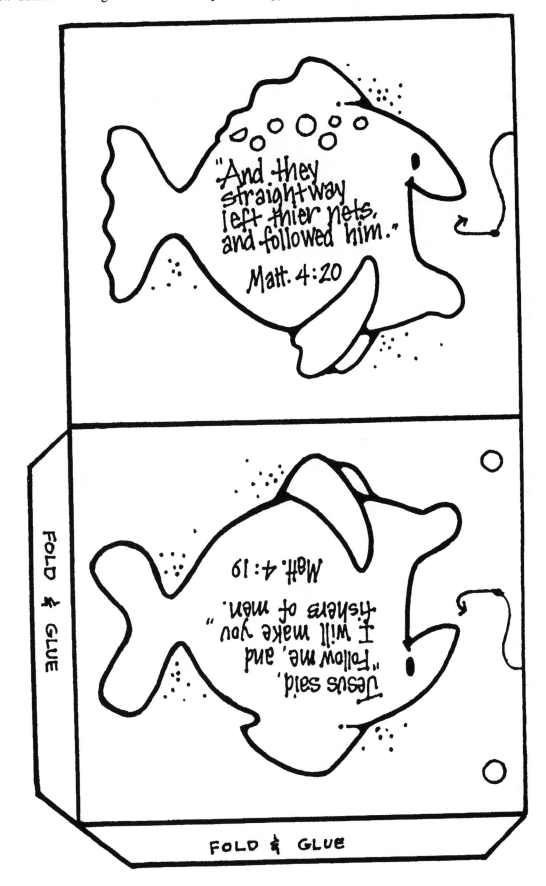

FOLD & GLUE

FOLD & GLUE

"And they straightway left thier nets, and followed him."

Matt. 4:20

Jesus said, "Follow me, and I will make you fishers of men."

Matt. 4:19

**PATTERN:** Fish Sticks sack for Thought Treat ♥ Copy on cardstock paper.

Something fishy is going on here!

Six little fishies
in a swimming game...
Find two fish
that look the same!

Jesus and the Apostles ate...

FISH FISH FISH FISH

FOLD & GLUE

FOLD & GLUE

# FISH-IONARY CERTIFICATE
## for Being a Disciple of Jesus Christ

Awarded to _____

on _____

(date you completed the "Fishers of Men" Search and Ponder cards)

Below each fish, write ways you can be a missionary to tell others about the gospel of Jesus Christ.

EXAMPLE

TEACHER

SPECIAL WITNESS

**PATTERN:** BONUS MOTIVATORS glue-on stickers for completing the "Fishers of Men" Search and Ponder cards (glue in notebooks, treasure boxes, journals, or tape on the mirror) ♥ Copy one for each guest.

### I Can Follow the Example of Jesus

### I Can Teach Others About Jesus

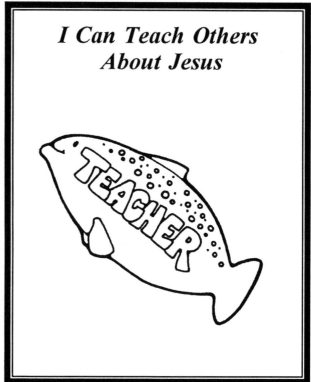

### I Can Be a Special Witness of Jesus Christ

### Thank You, Jesus, for Sending Me the Holy Ghost to Guide Me

PLACE ACTIVITIES
IN FILE FOLDER:
Cut out and mount
label and checklist on
folder.

→
↓

New Testament

# The Gifts He Gave:
## Tell Me the Stories of Jesus

# SCRIPTURE ACTIVITY CHECKLIST
### The Gifts He Gave: Tell Me the Stories of Jesus

PAGES:

At Christmas time, we honor the birth of Jesus by giving gifts to others. By giving gifts, we show our love for others and for Jesus.

Jesus showed love for us by giving gifts that we can enjoy all year. These gifts are the stories he told. They are called parables. The apostles recorded them, and we can find them in the books of the New Testament.

Let's learn about the gifts he gave. Tell me the stories of Jesus.

**DO AHEAD:**
- ☐ Copy patterns .... 62-86
- ☐ Create gift invitation with elephant tag ....... 52
- ☐ Gather supplies*

PAGES:

## SEARCH and PONDER:

- ☐ SEARCH & PONDER cards ......................... 53-54
- ☐ SCRIPTURE SHOW-AND-TELL: Rehearse cue cards for presentation: The Gifts He Gave: Tell Me the Stories of Jesus ... 55-58

## PLAY: SUPER SCRIPTURE ACTIVITY Choices

- ☐ SCRIPTURE SHOW-AND-TELL presentation
- ☐ GAME: Parables in a Pocket: Stories of Jesus match game ...... 59
- ☐ SONGS:
  - ○ "Tell Me the Stories of Jesus," page 57**
  - ○ "I Think When I Read That Sweet Story," page 56**
  - ○ "Little Lambs So White and Fair," page 58*

- ☐ FAVORS and PRIZES: .................. 60
  - ○ Picture a Perfect Parable poster & glue-on stickers
  - ○ Purple or White Elephant gift exchange
- ☐ THOUGHT TREATS: .................. 61
  - ○ Unforgettable Parable Cupcakes with elephant sign
  - ○ Purple Perfect Parable Punch with cup label
- ☐ BONUS MOTIVATORS: .......... 80, 81-86

*SUPPLIES:
Pattern copies, scissors, crayons or markers, purple yarn or ribbon, toothpicks, 8-ounce paper cups, aluminum foil, and Thought Treats

SUPPLEMENTAL READING--New Testament Stories**: The Good Samaritan, Jesus Tells Three Stories: The Lost Sheep, The Lost Coin, and The Lost Son, Ten Young Women, and The Talents

**Children's Songbook and New Testament Stories are published by The Church of Jesus Christ of Latter-day Saints, Salt Lake City, Utah.

**PATTERNS:** Invitation and White Elephant Gift Exchange tag
**YOU'LL NEED:** Copy of patterns below on violet or purple cardstock paper for each guest, scissors, crayons, paper punch, and purple yarn or ribbon  ♥ **INVITATION:** Fill in details

Cut out the tag and attach to a white elephant gift to exchange!

♥ **WHITE ELEPHANT GIFT EXCHANGE TAG:** Punch a hole in the elephant tag (right), and in the invitation (below). Tie elephant to invitation with purple yarn or ribbon (elephant instructs guests to bring a white elephant or used gift to the SUPER SCRIPTURE ACTIVITY. Instruct guests to wrap gift and tie the elephant tag to the gift. See instructions on page 60 for the gift exchange.

Please come to a
SCRIPTURE ACTIVITY!
and learn of the gifts Jesus gave.
To: _____
Date: _____
Time: _____
Place: _____

## Scripture SEARCH and PONDER:

♥ Copy two sets of SEARCH and PONDER cards below on colored cardstock paper. ♥ Cut out cards.
- ◻ <u>Use Set #1</u> for Daily Devotionals.
- ◻ OPTION: Make a second set of cards to play The New Testament Game--Spotlighting the Life of Jesus. (This game is found on pages 59-60 of SUPER SCRIPTURE ACTIVITIES--NEW TESTAMENT, by Mary H. Ross and Jennette Guymon. Copy each set of cards a different color to identify quickly, i.e. copy this set violet or purple.)

---

### SEARCH #1
The Stories of Jesus

**Parable: The Lost Sheep**

"What man of you, having an hundred sheep, if he lose _ _ _ _ of them, doth not leave the ninety and nine in the wilderness, and go after that which is lost, until he _ _ _ _ _ it?
And when he hath found it, he layeth it on his shoulders, rejoicing." (Luke 15:4-5)

---

### SEARCH #2
The Stories of Jesus

**Parable: The Talents**

"For the kingdom of heaven is as a man ... who called his own servants, and delivered unto them his goods. And unto one he gave _ _ _ _ _ talents, to another _ _ _, and to another _ _ _: ... every man ... took his journey. Then he that had received 5 talents ... made them over 5 talents. And likewise he that had received 2, he also gained other 2. But he that had received 1 went and digged in the earth, and hid his lord's money."
(Matthew 25:14-18)

---

### SEARCH #3
The Stories of Jesus

**Parable: Ten Young Women**

"The kingdom of heaven be likened unto ten virgins, which took their lamps ... to meet the bridegroom. And five of them were _ _ _ _ _ and five were _ _ _ _ _ _ _. They that were foolish took their lamps, and took no oil with them: But the wise took oil in their vessels with their lamps. And the foolish said unto the wise, ... our lamps are gone out ... And while they went to buy, the bride-groom came ... and the door was shut."(Matthew 25:1-4, 8, 10)

---

### SEARCH #4
The Stories of Jesus

**Parable: The Lost Son**

"A certain man had two sons: And the younger ... said to his father, ... give me the portion of goods that falleth to me. And he divided unto them his living. And ... the younger son ... wasted his substance with _ _ _ _ _ _ _ _ _ _ living. And when he had spent all ... he began to be in want. The son said ... Father, I have sinned against heaven, and in thy sight ... But the father said ... For this my son was dead, and is alive again; he was lost, and is found." (Luke 15:11-14, 21-24)

---

### SEARCH #5
The Stories of Jesus

**Parable: The Mustard Seed**

Jesus said that the kingdom of God is like "a grain of mustard seed, which a man took, and cast into his garden; and it _ _ _ _ _, and waxed a great tree; and the fowls of the air lodged in the branches of it." (Luke 13:18)

Jesus also said that the mustard seed "is the _ _ _ _ _ of all seeds: but when it is grown, it is the _ _ _ _ _ _ _ _ among herbs, and becometh a tree." (Matthew 13:31-32)

---

### SEARCH #6
The Stories of Jesus

**Parable: The Good Samaritan**

"And Jesus ... said, A certain man went down from Jerusalem to Jericho, and fell among _ _ _ _ _ _ _, which stripped him of his raiment, and wounded him, and departed, leaving him half dead. And ... a certain priest ... passed by on the other side. And likewise a Levite ... passed by ... But a certain Samaritan, as he journeyed, ... saw him, he had compassion on him. And he went to him, and bound up his wounds ... and took _ _ _ _ of him." (Luke 10:30-34)

**PATTERNS:** PONDER Cards #1-6

## PONDER #1
The Stories of Jesus

**Parable:  The Lost Sheep**

Jesus told the Pharisees about the shepherd who had 100 sheep and lost one.  He left the 99 and found the 1.

What did Jesus say that made him very happy? (Luke 15:6-7)

Joy shall be in heaven over one sinner that

_ _ _ _ _ _ _ _ _ .

## PONDER #2
The Stories of Jesus

**Parable:  The Talents**

What happend to the servant who buried his talent?
(Matthew 25:25, 28-29)

CHECK ONE:

☐ He was given more talents.

☐ His talents were given away to the one who had earned ten talents.

## PONDER #3
The Stories of Jesus

**Parable:  Ten Young Women**

What happened to the foolish young maidens who did not bring oil to light their lamps?
(Matthew 25:10)

They went to buy oil and the wedding door was _ _ _ _ .
They were too late.

## PONDER #4
The Stories of Jesus

**Parable:  The Lost Son**

Why did the younger son desire to come back home?
(Luke 15:17)

His father had _ _ _ _ _ enough to spare.

. . . . . . . . . . . . . . . . . . . . . . . .

What did the younger son say to the father? (Luke 15:21)
"I have _ _ _ _ _ _ against heaven, and in thy sight, and am no more worthy to be called thy _ _ _ ."

## PONDER #5
The Stories of Jesus

**Parable:  The Mustard Seed**

What did Jesus say the kingdom of God was like?  What did he compare it to?
A grain of _ _ _ _ _ _ _
_ _ _ _ that can grow into a
great _ _ _ _ .  (Luke 13:19)

The mustard seed is the smallest of all seeds, but when it is grown it is the greatest of all herbs.  We too can grow and become great by living the commandments.  We can become part of God's kingdom as we "plant" good thoughts and deeds. (Matthew 13:31-32.)

## PONDER #6
The Stories of Jesus

**Parable:  The Good Samaritan**

Who passed by the Jew who was beaten and left half dead on the road? (Luke 10:31-32)
a _ _ _ _ _ _ _ and a
_ _ _ _ _ _ _

. . . . . . . . . . . . . . . . . . . . . . . .

Who helped him to the inn, clothed him and fed him?
(Luke 10:33-34)

The good

_ _ _ _ _ _ _ _ _ _ _ _ .

# Scripture Show-and-Tell

## The Gifts He Gave: Tell Me the Stories of Jesus poster

♥     Copy and cut out cue cards that follow.

♥     Copy and color Jesus, Jesus' hands, and gift pictures #1-6 (patterns on pages 62-69).

All patterns can be posted on a board or poster paper (see layout below).

---

SEARCH, PONDER, and PLAY

**PRESENTATION PLAN:**
**Cards #1-6**

**Scripture
Show-and-Tell**
**The Gifts He Gave:**
Tell Me the Stories of Jesus

**SHOW:**                                        **TELL: Cue Cards #1-6**

Jesus and hands (see card #1)

| | | |
|---|---|---|
| Gift #1 | PARABLE: The Lost Sheep . . . . . . . . . . . . . . . | Card #1 |
| Gift #2 | PARABLE: The Talents . . . . . . . . . . . . . . . . . . | Card #2 |
| Gift #3 | PARABLE: Ten Young Women . . . . . . . . . . . . . | Card #3 |
| Gift #4 | PARABLE: The Lost Son . . . . . . . . . . . . . . . . . | Card #4 |
| Gift #5 | PARABLE: The Mustard Seed . . . . . . . . . . . . . | Card #5 |
| Gift #6 | PARABLE: The Good Samaritan . . . . . . . . . . . | Card #6 |

CUT OUT cards #1-6 to rehearse Show-and-Tell presentation.

SEARCH, PONDER, and PLAY
Jesus Told Parables:  The Lost Sheep

**Place Jesus and hands on board and say:**

Jesus was a great teacher.  He taught in parables or stories.  Each parable will tell you how you can get to heaven.

**Place Gift #1 (Lost Sheep) on board and say:**

Parable of The Lost Sheep:  There was a good shepherd who had 100 sheep.  One day, when he counted the sheep, one was lost.

 He counted only 99 sheep, so he went out to look for the lost one.  He wanted to save it from the wolves and from starving.

He searched until he found it.  He was happy as he picked it up and carried it home on his shoulders.  When he got home, he told his friends and neighbors that he found the lost lamb.

Jesus told the Pharisees that this story was about him.  He is like the good shepherd, and sinners are like the lost sheep.  Jesus said he came to save the lost sheep, to save people from their sins.

Jesus said he is very happy when he finds sinners who repent.

**JESUS WANTS US TO FIND AND HELP THOSE IN NEED.**

Scripture Show-and-Tell
**Cue Card #1**
Gifts He Gave

SEARCH, PONDER, and PLAY
PARABLE:  The Talents

**Place Gift #2 (Talents) on board and say:**

Parable of The Talents:  A man had three servants.  He gave each servant some money.  Each coin was called a talent.

He gave the first servant <u>five</u> talents, and the second servant <u>two</u> talents, and to the third servant he gave <u>one</u> talent.  Each servant went to another land.

The first servant with <u>five</u> talents worked hard and earned <u>five</u> more talents.  He had <u>ten</u> talents to bring back.

The second servant with <u>two</u> talents worked hard and earned <u>two</u> more talents.  He had <u>four</u> talents to bring back.

The third servant was afraid he would lose the <u>one</u> talent he was given, so he buried it in the ground.  When it was time to go back, he dug it up and brought back the <u>one</u> talent he was given.

When the servants reported back to the man who gave them the talents, the man was happy.  The two servants had worked hard and increased their talents, so he gave them more talents.  He was angry with the third servant who buried his talent.  He took his talent away and gave it to another.  Then he sent the lazy servant away.

**JESUS WANTS US TO WORK HARD TO INCREASE OUR TALENTS.**

Scripture Show-and-Tell
**Cue Card #2**
The Gifts He Gave

SEARCH, PONDER, and PLAY
PARABLE:  Ten Young Women

Place Gift #3 (Ten Women) on board and say:

Scripture Show-and-Tell
**Cue Card #3**
The Gifts He Gave

Ten Young Women:  Ten young women were going to help at a wedding.

Five women were wise, and they took extra oil to light their lamps.  The other five were foolish.  They did not take extra oil in case their lamps went out.

They all waited for the bridegroom to let them in.  It was late, and they fell asleep.  At midnight it was time to go in.

The five women who were wise had enough oil to light their lamps, but the five who were foolish could not light their lamps.  They had to leave to buy more oil.

While they were gone, the wedding began.  The five wise women were allowed to go in, but the five foolish women were late and the doors were closed.

Jesus is like the bridegroom, and we are like these young women.
**JESUS WANTS US TO BE PREPARED, AS HE WILL COME AGAIN.**

SEARCH, PONDER, and PLAY
PARABLE:  The Lost Son

Place Gift #4 (Lost Son) on board and say:

Scripture Show-and-Tell
**Cue Card #4**
The Gifts He Gave

Parable of The Lost Son:  A man had two sons who would receive his money when he died.  The younger son wanted his money now.

The father gave the younger son the money.  The son left home and sinned.  He did not obey God's commandments.  He spent all his money, and had no money to buy food.

He found a job feeding pigs, and was so hungry, he wanted to eat the food the pigs were eating.  He thought of his family and their food.

He knew he had sinned, but he wanted to go home.  He went home to repent and ask his father to forgive him.

His father saw him coming and threw his arms around him and kissed him.  The son told his father that he was sorry for not obeying him, and for not obeying God.  The father had his servants bring the boy new clothes, shoes, and a ring for his finger.  He had a big dinner for his son to tell everyone how happy he was that his son was home.

The older son was angry, and told the father that he had obeyed him; yet, he had never received a special dinner in his honor.  The father told the older son that everything he had would belong to him someday.  But the younger son had gone away and come home again; he was a sinner and had repented.  **JESUS WANTS US TO REPENT AND TO FORGIVE OTHERS.**

SEARCH, PONDER, and PLAY
PARABLE: The Mustard Seed

**Place Gift #5 (Mustard Seed) on board and say:**

Scripture Show-and-Tell
## Cue Card #5
**The Gifts He Gave**

Parable of The Mustard Seed: The ruler of the Jerusalem synagogue or church asked Jesus, "What is the kingdom of God like?"

Jesus said: "*It is like a grain of mustard seed, which a man took, and cast into his garden; and it grew, and waxed a great tree; and the fowls of the air lodged in the branches of it.*" (Luke 13:18)

We too can be like this man who planted a mustard seed. We can plant good thoughts in our minds as we read the scriptures. We can grow as we keep the commandments.

Jesus also said that the mustard seed "*is the least of all seeds: but when it is grown, it is the greatest among herbs.*" (Matthew 13:32)

We can grow with good thoughts and good deeds, like the mustard seed.
We can grow tall in spirit as well as stature, like the seed that grew into a 10-15 foot tree.

## JESUS WANTS US TO PLANT GOOD THOUGHTS AND GROW TOWARD HEAVEN.

---

SEARCH, PONDER, and PLAY
PARABLE: The Good Samaritan

**Place Gift #6 (Samaritan) on board and say:**

Scripture Show-and-Tell
## Cue Card #6
**The Gifts He Gave**

Parable of The Good Samaritan: A leader of the Jews asked Jesus how to get to heaven. Jesus asked him what the scriptures said. The man said to love God and love your neighbor. Jesus said he was right. Then the leader asked Jesus, "Who is my neighbor?"

Jesus told the story of a Jew walking along the road. Some thieves stopped him, beat him, and took his clothes. He was left along the road, almost dead.

A Jewish priest came by and saw that he was hurt, yet he passed by, leaving him alone.

A Levite man came by and saw that he was hurt, but he walked by on the other side of the road, leaving him alone.

Then a Samaritan man came along. Samaritans and Jews did not get along. The Samaritan knew the man was a Jew, but he stopped to help him. He put clothes on the man and took him to an inn, and took care of him until the next day. When he left, he gave money to the man in the inn to take care of him.

## JESUS WANTS US TO BE KIND TO OTHERS AND HELP THEM.

These are just a few of the gifts Jesus gave. Search the scriptures for more stories and blessings.

SEARCH, PONDER, and PLAY

**GAME:  Parables in a Pocket:
Stories of Jesus match**

**GAME**
**The Gifts He Gave**

**OBJECTIVE:**
Make each parable complete by placing wordstrips #1-6 in the right parable pocket (gift picture).  Enjoy reading each completed parable together.

**YOU'LL NEED:**
1. Copy Parables in a Pocket sign on page 70 and gift patterns used for the Scripture Show-and-Tell on pages 64-69.  Reduce patterns 50% as you copy them on cardstock paper.
2. Copy "Parables in a pocket" sign and parable wordstrips (#1-6) on pages 70-76 on cardstock paper.
3. Supplies:  Poster paper, scissors, glue, and crayons or markers.

**HOW TO MAKE GAME BOARD & GAME:**
1. Color and cut out gift pictures, sign and wordstrips #1-6.
2. Cut a slit at the top of each gift to slide in wordstrips #1-6.
3. Glue gifts to a piece of poster paper on sides and bottom (1/4 inch), leaving the center open for a pocket.

**HOW TO PLAY GAME:**
1. Mix parable wordstrips #1-6 from each parable in a bowl or box to draw from.
2. Divide into two teams with two players from each team helping each other.
3. Match a Parable:  Team players take turns drawing a parable wordstrip, reading it, and placing it in the matching parable pocket.
4. Read Parables in Pocket:  As soon as wordstrips #1-6 are placed in a pocket, the pocket is full.  The team that placed the last wordstrip pulls out wordstrips #1-6 and reads the parable aloud.  If time permits, play until all parables are read.
　　　NOTE:  This activity can be continued.  Award the Picture a Perfect
　　　Parable poster (with glue-on stickers) as a prize (see page 60, 77-78).

SEARCH, PONDER, and PLAY

## PICTURE A PERFECT PARABLE
### "Gifts He Gave" poster
(with glue-on stickers)

**FAVOR or PRIZE**
The Gifts He Gave

**OBJECTIVE:** Review parables of Jesus.

**YOU'LL NEED:** Copy of the "Gifts He Gave" poster on page 77 and the glue-on sticker patterns on page 78 for each guest, crayons or markers, and glue

**DECORATE POSTER WITH GLUE-ON STICKERS:**
1. Cut out stickers.
2. Glue stickers on "Gifts He Gave" poster over the matching parable.

---

SEARCH, PONDER, and PLAY

## PURPLE (White) ELEPHANT GIFT EXCHANGE

**FAVOR or PRIZE**
The Gifts He Gave

**OBJECTIVE:** Guests bring a used gift, known as a white elephant, to exchange.

**DO AHEAD:** Copy and cut out elephant pattern on page 52 on violet or purple paper for each guest. Punch and tie to invitation with purple yarn or ribbon. Attach to invitation. When sending invitations, instruct guests to wrap gift and tie purple elephant tag on gift.

### GIFT EXCHANGE:
1. Place wrapped gifts in the center of the room and sit in a circle. Guests take turns choosing a gift from the center.
2. Before opening gift, guest says: "PURPLE ELEPHANTS PICK PERFECT PARABLES." Then guest names his/her favorite parable of Jesus listed on page 55.
3. Then guest opens gift, taking off the purple elephant tag.
4. Play until all gifts are opened. End activity by saying: "PURPLE ELEPHANTS LOVE PERFECT PARABLES." Allow guests to trade gifts if they wish.

SEARCH, PONDER, and PLAY

## UNFORGETTABLE PARABLE CUPCAKES
(with parable wordstrips baked inside)

**You'll Need:** Copy of elephant sign that reads "Elephants <u>never</u> forget the parables of Jesus!" on page 79 on violet or purple cardstock paper, a parable wordstrip from pages 71-76 (reduced 50%) on lightweight violet or purple paper, two toothpicks for each guest, cake mix and frosting, cupcake liners, and aluminum foil

**TO MAKE:**
1. Roll up a wordstrip and cover with aluminum foil.
2. Drop a wrapped wordstrip into cupcake liners.
3. Mix cupcake batter and pour into cupcake liners 3/4 full (covering wrapped parable wordstrip).
4. Bake cupcakes at 350° for 15-20 minutes.
5. Frost cupcakes and top with elephant sign (inserted with toothpicks).

**ACTIVITY:** Read the scripture above and talk about the gifts Jesus has given you. The most important gift is eternal life. Others are: Prayer, scriptures, example, priesthood, healing, commandments, plan for happiness, love, and parables. Then have each guest read the parable wordstrip inside cupcake and guess which parable it goes with (parables listed on page 55).

---

SEARCH, PONDER, and PLAY

## PURPLE PERFECT PARABLE PUNCH:
(purple punch served in purple cup with perfect parables listed)

**You'll Need:** Copy of paper cup label on page 80 on violet or purple cardstock paper, an 8-ounce cup, purple punch for each guest, scissors, crayons or markers, and glue

**To Make Parable Punch:**
1. Color and cut out label.
2. Glue label on an 8-ounce paper cup.
3. Pour purple punch and serve.

**ACTIVITY:** Read paper cup label and scripture above. As you sip your Purple Perfect Parable Punch, name your favorite parable.

**PATTERN:**  Jesus for Scripture Show-and-Tell  ♥ Copy on cardstock paper.

**PATTERN:**  Hands of Jesus for Scripture Show-and-Tell   ♥ Copy on cardstock paper.

**PATTERN:** Gift #1  PARABLE:  The Lost Sheep for Scripture Show-and-Tell  ♥ Copy on cardstock paper.

**PATTERN:** Gift #2 PARABLE: The Talents for Scripture Show-and-Tell ♥ Copy on cardstock paper.

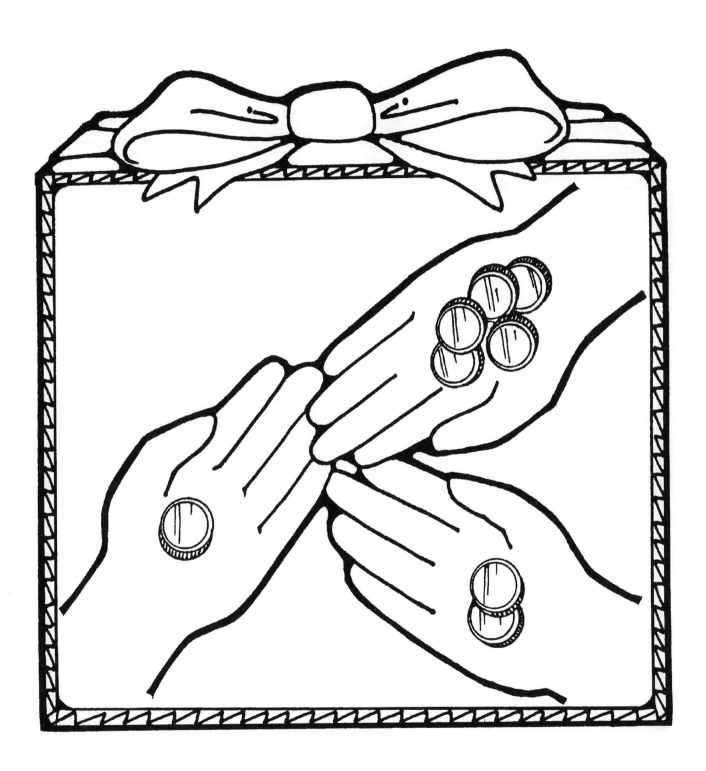

**PATTERN:**  Gift #3  PARABLE:  Ten Young Women for Scripture Show-and-Tell  ♥ Copy on cardstock paper.

**PATTERN:**  Gift #4 PARABLE:  The Lost Son for Scripture Show-and-Tell  ♥  Copy on cardstock paper.

**PATTERN:** Gift #5 PARABLE: The Mustard Seed for Scripture Show-and-Tell ♥ Copy on cardstock paper.

**PATTERN:** Gift #6  PARABLE:  The Good Samaritan for Scripture Show-and-Tell  ♥ Copy on cardstock paper.

**PATTERN:** "Parables in a Pocket" sign for Parables in a Pocket game ♥ Copy one on colored cardstock.

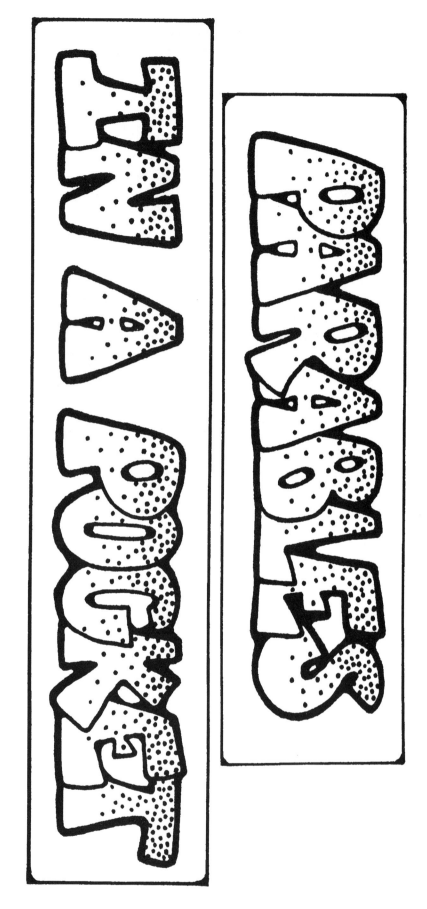

**PATTERN:**  Parable (The Lost Sheep) word strips for Parables in a Pocket game  ♥ Copy one on colored cardstock.

**6**

JESUS WANTS US TO FIND AND HELP THOSE IN NEED.

**1**

There was a good shepherd who had 100 sheep. One day, when he counted the sheep, one was lost.

**2**

He counted only 99 sheep, so he went out to look for the lost one. He wanted to save it from the wolves and from starving.

**3**

He searched until he found it. He was happy as he picked it up and carried it home on his shoulders. When he got home, he told his friends and neighbors that he found the lost lamb.

**4**

Jesus told the Pharisees that this story was about him. He is like the good shepherd, and sinners are like the lost sheep. Jesus said he came to save the lost sheep, to save people from their sins.

**5**

Jesus said he is very happy when he finds sinners who repent.

**PATTERN:**  Parable (The Talents) word strips for Parables in a Pocket game  ♥ Copy one on colored cardstock.

| | |
|---|---|
| **6** | **1** |

JESUS WANTS US TO WORK HARD TO INCREASE OUR TALENTS.

A man had three servants. He gave each servant some money. Each coin was called a talent.

He gave the first servant five talents, and the second servant he gave two talents, and to the third servant he gave one talent. Each servant went to another land.

**2**

The first servant with five talents worked hard and earned five more talents. He had ten talents to bring back.

**3**

The second servant with two talents worked hard and earned two more talents. He had four talents to bring back.

**4**

The third servant was afraid he would lose the one talent he was given, so he buried it in the ground. When it was time to go back, he dug it up and brought back the one talent he was given.

**5**

When the servants reported back to the man who gave them the talents, the man was happy. The two servants had worked hard and increased their talents, so he gave them more talents.

He was angry with the third servant who buried his talent. He took his talent away and gave it to another. Then he sent the lazy servant away.

**PATTERN:** Parable (10 Young Women) word strips for Parables in a Pocket game ♥ Copy one on colored cardstock.

**1**

Ten young women were going to help at a wedding.

Five women were wise, and they took extra oil to light their lamps. The other five were foolish. They did not take extra oil in case their lamps went out.

**2**

They all waited for the bridegroom to let them in. It was late, and they fell asleep. At midnight it was time to go in.

**3**

The five women who were wise had enough oil to light their lamps, but the five who were foolish could not light their lamps. They had to leave to buy more oil.

**4**

While they were gone, the wedding began. The five wise women were allowed to go in, but the five foolish women were late and the doors were closed.

**5**

Jesus is the bridegroom, and we are like these young women.

**6**

JESUS WANTS US TO BE PREPARED, AS HE WILL COME AGAIN.

**PATTERN:** Parable (The Lost Son) word strips for Parables in a Pocket game ♥ Copy one on colored cardstock.

**6**

**JESUS WANTS US TO REPENT AND TO FORGIVE OTHERS.**

**1**

A man had two sons who would receive his money when he died. The younger son wanted his money now. The father gave the younger son the money. The son left home and sinned. He did not obey God's commandments. He spent all his money, and had no money to buy food.

**2**

He found a job feeding pigs, and was so hungry, he wanted to eat the food the pigs were eating. He thought of his family and their food.

**3**

He knew he had sinned, but he wanted to go home. He went home to repent and ask his father to forgive him.

**4**

His father saw him coming and threw his arms around him and kissed him. The son told his father that he had obeyed him; yet, he had never received a special dinner in his honor. The father told the older son that everything he had would belong to him someday. But the younger son had gone away and come home again; he was a sinner and had repented.

His father saw him coming and threw his arms around him and kissed him. The son told his father that he was sorry for not obeying him, and for not obeying God. The father had his servants bring the boy new clothes, shoes, and a ring for his finger. He had a big dinner for his son, to tell everyone how happy he was that his son was home.

**5**

The older son was angry, and told the father that he had obeyed him; yet, he had never received a special dinner in his honor. The father told the older son that everything he had would belong to him someday. But the younger son had gone away and come home again; he was a sinner and had repented.

The Gifts He Gave: Tell Me the Stories of Jesus

**PATTERN:** Parable (The Mustard Seed) word strips for Parables in a Pocket game ♥ Copy one on colored cardstock.

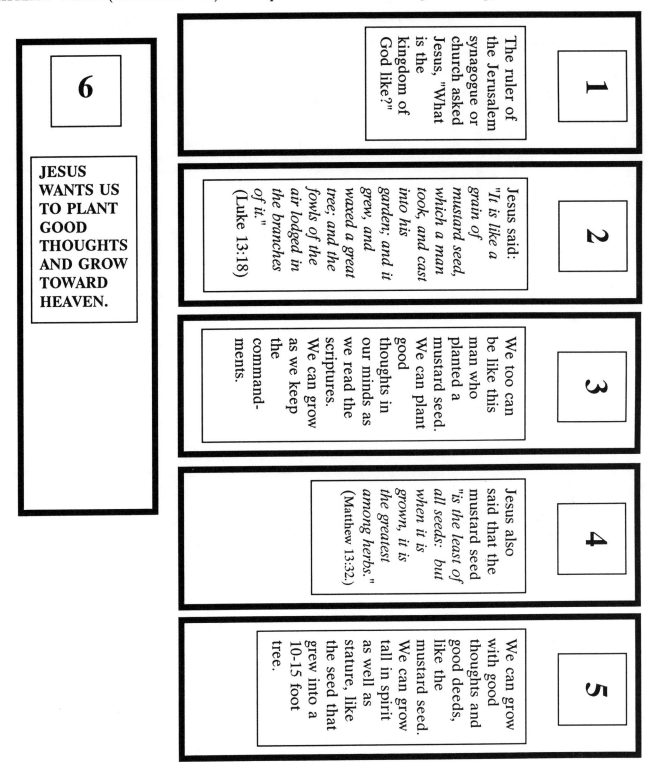

**6**

JESUS WANTS US TO PLANT GOOD THOUGHTS AND GROW TOWARD HEAVEN.

**1**

The ruler of the Jerusalem synagogue or church asked Jesus, "What is the kingdom of God like?"

**2**

Jesus said: "It is like a grain of mustard seed, which a man took, and cast into his garden; and it grew, and waxed a great tree; and the fowls of the air lodged in the branches of it." (Luke 13:18)

**3**

We too can be like this man who planted a mustard seed. We can plant good thoughts in our minds as we read the scriptures. We can grow as we keep the commandments.

**4**

Jesus also said that the mustard seed "is the least of all seeds: but when it is grown, it is the greatest among herbs." (Matthew 13:32.)

**5**

We can grow with good thoughts and good deeds, like the mustard seed. We can grow tall in spirit as well as stature, like the seed that grew into a 10-15 foot tree.

75

**PATTERN:**   Parable (Good Samaritan) word strips for Parables in a Pocket game  ♥ Copy one on colored cardstock.

6

JESUS
WANTS US
TO BE KIND
TO
OTHERS.

1

A leader of the Jews asked Jesus how to get to heaven. Jesus asked him what the scriptures said. The man said to love God and love your neighbor. Jesus said he was right. Then the leader asked Jesus, "Who is my neighbor?"

2

Jesus told the story of a Jew walking along the road. Some thieves stopped him, beat him, and took his clothes. He was left along the road, almost dead.

3

A Jewish priest came by and saw that he was hurt, yet he passed by, leaving him alone.

4

A Levite man came by, and saw that he was hurt, but he walked by on the other side of the road, leaving him alone.

5

Then a Samaritan man came along. Samaritans and Jews did not get along. The Samaritan knew the man was a Jew, but he stopped to help him. He put clothes on the man and took him to an inn, and took care of him until the next day. When he left, he gave money to the man in the inn to take care of him.

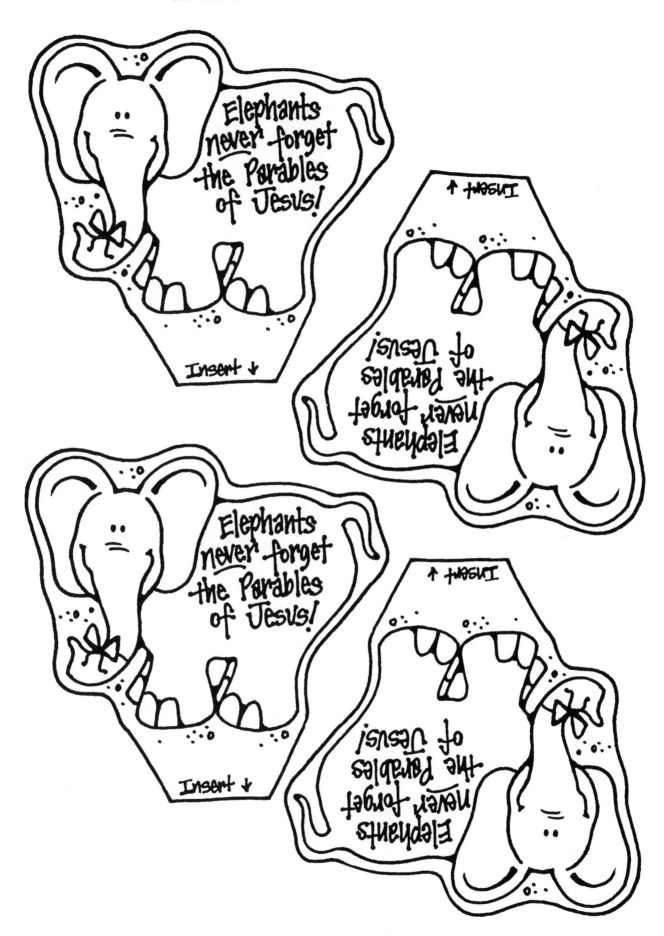

**PATTERN:** ♥ Copy one for each guest on  violet or purple cardstock paper.
**PURPLE PERFECT PARABLE PUNCH** cup label
**BONUS MOTIVATOR --** Rewards for completing
"The Stories of Jesus" Search and Ponder Cards:
○ Certificate:  PURPLE ELEPHANTS LOVE
PERFECT PARABLES
○ Color-and-Learn Posters on pages 81-86 to learn
the parables of Jesus.  Post on wall or mirror.

# Purple Elephants Love Perfect PARABLES

## Certificate Awarded

To: _____

on _____
(date you completed "The Stories of Jesus"
Search and Ponder cards)

# CONGRATULATIONS
## on a
## Perfect Performance!

# Parable of the Lost Sheep

Jesus was a great teacher. He taught in parables or stories.
Each parable will tell you how you can get to heaven.

## PARABLE OF THE LOST SHEEP (Luke 15:1-7):

There was a good shepherd who had 100 sheep. One day, when he counted the sheep, one was lost.

He counted only 99 sheep, so he went out to look for the lost one. He wanted to save it from the wolves and from starving.

He searched until he found it. He was happy as he picked it up, and carried it home on his shoulders. When he got home, he told his friends and neighbors that he found the lost lamb.

Jesus told the Pharisees that this story was about him. He is like the good shepherd, and sinners are like the lost sheep. Jesus said he came to save the lost sheep, to save people from their sins.

Jesus said he is very happy when he finds sinners who repent.

**JESUS WANTS US TO FIND AND HELP THOSE IN NEED.**

# Parable of the Talents

**Matthew 25:14-29**

A man had three servants. He gave each servant some money. Each coin was called a talent.

He gave the first servant <u>five</u> talents, and the second servant <u>two</u> talents, and to the third servant he gave <u>one</u> talent. Each servant went to another land.

The first servant with <u>five</u> talents worked hard and earned <u>five</u> more talents. He had <u>ten</u> talents to bring back.

The second servant with <u>two</u> talents worked hard and earned <u>two</u> more talents. He had <u>four</u> talents to bring back.

The third servant was afraid he would lose the <u>one</u> talent he was given, so he buried it in the ground. When it was time to go back, he dug it up and brought back the <u>one</u> talent he was given.

When the servants reported back to the man who gave them the talents, the man was happy. The two servants had worked hard and increased their talents, so he gave them more talents. He was angry with the third servant who buried his talent. He took his talent away and gave it to another. Then he sent the lazy servant away.

**JESUS WANTS US TO WORK HARD TO INCREASE OUR TALENTS.**

# Parable of the Ten Women

## Matthew 25:1-13

Ten young women were going to help at a wedding.

Five women were wise, and they took extra oil to light their lamps. The other five were foolish. They did not take extra oil in case their lamps went out.

They all waited for the bridegroom to let them in. It was late, and they fell asleep. At midnight it was time to go in.

The five women who were wise had enough oil to light their lamps, but the five who were foolish could not light their lamps. They had to leave to buy more oil.

While they were gone, the wedding began. The five wise women were allowed to go in, but the five foolish women were late and the doors were closed.

Jesus is like the bridegroom, and we are like these young women.

**JESUS WANTS US TO BE PREPARED, AS HE WILL COME AGAIN.**

# Parable of the Lost Son

## Luke 15:11-32

A man had two sons who would receive his money when he died. The younger son wanted his money now.

The father gave the younger son the money. The son left home and sinned. He did not obey God's commandments. He spent all his money, and had no money to buy food.

He found a job feeding pigs, and was so hungry, he wanted to eat the food the pigs were eating. He thought of his family and their food.

He knew he had sinned, but he wanted to go home. He went home to repent and ask his father to forgive him.

His father saw him coming and threw his arms around him and kissed him. The son told his father that he was sorry for not obeying him, and for not obeying God. The father had his servants bring the boy new clothes, shoes, and a ring for his finger. He had a big dinner for his son to tell everyone how happy he was that his son was home.

The older son was angry, and told the father that he had obeyed him; yet, he had never received a special dinner in his honor. The father told the older son that everything he had would belong to him someday. But the younger son had gone away and come home again; he was a sinner and had repented.

**JESUS WANTS US TO REPENT AND TO FORGIVE OTHERS.**

# Parable of the Mustard Seed

## Matthew 13:31-32

The ruler of the Jerusalem synagogue or church asked Jesus, "What is the kingdom of God like?"

Jesus said: *"It is like a grain of mustard seed, which a man took, and cast into his garden; and it grew, and waxed a great tree; and the fowls of the air lodged in the branches of it."* (Luke 13:18)

We too can be like this man who planted a mustard seed. We can plant good thoughts in our minds as we read the scriptures. We can grow as we keep the commandments.

Jesus also said that the mustard seed *"is the least of all seeds: but when it is grown, it is the greatest among herbs."* (Matthew 13:32)

We can grow with good thoughts and good deeds, like the mustard seed.
We can grow tall in spirit as well as stature, like the seed that grew into a 10-15 foot tree.

**JESUS WANTS US TO PLANT GOOD THOUGHTS
AND GROW TOWARD HEAVEN.**

# Parable of the Good Samaritan

## Luke 10:30-34

A leader of the Jews asked Jesus how to get to heaven. Jesus asked him what the scriptures said. The man said to love God and love your neighbor. Jesus said he was right. Then the leader asked Jesus, "Who is my neighbor?"

Jesus told the story of a Jew walking along the road. Some thieves stopped him, beat him, and took his clothes. He was left along the road, almost dead.

A Jewish priest came by and saw that he was hurt, yet he passed by, leaving him alone.

A Levite man came by and saw that he was hurt, but he walked by on the other side of the road, leaving him alone.

Then a Samaritan man came along. Samaritans and Jews did not get along. The Samaritan knew the man was a Jew, but he stopped to help him. He put clothes on the man and took him to an inn, and took care of him until the next day. When he left, he gave money to the man in the inn to take care of him.

**JESUS WANTS US TO BE KIND TO OTHERS AND HELP THEM.**

**Mary H. Ross**, Author and
**Jennette Guymon**, Illustrator
are also creators of:

**SUPER SCRIPTURE ACTIVITIES:**
New Testament--I'm Trying to Be Like Jesus
New Testament--Jesus Is My Friend,
(detailed below)
and
**PRIMARY PARTNERS:** A-Z Activities
to Make Learning Fun for Nursery and Age 3
- Nursery/Sunbeams -
(detailed on the following page)

**MARY H. ROSS**, Author
Mary Ross is an energetic mother and Primary teacher who loves to help children have a good time while they learn. She is a published author and columnist and has studied acting, modeling, and voice. Her varied interests include writing, creating activities, children's parties, and cooking. Mary and her husband, Paul, live with their daughter Jennifer in Sandy, Utah.
- Photos by Scott Hancock Provo, Utah

**JENNETTE GUYMON**, Illustrator
Jennette Guymon has studied graphic arts and illustration at Utah Valley State College and the University of Utah, and is currently employed with a commercial construction company. She served a mission to Japan and enjoys language, sports, reading, cooking, art, and freelance illustrating. Jennette lives in Salt Lake City, Utah and attends the Mount Olympus Third Ward.

Enjoy
**SUPER SCRIPTURE ACTIVITIES:**
**New Testament--I'm Trying to Be Like Jesus**

Also Enjoy
**SUPER SCRIPTURE ACTIVITIES:**
**New Testament--Jesus Is My Friend**

HEAVENLY TREASURES:
Follow the Straight and Narrow Path
SEEDS OF FAITH:
My Testimony Can Grow
IN HIS STEPS:
Spotlighting the Life of Jesus
CREATING ME:
I'm Trying to Be Like Jesus
CHOOSE THE RIGHT:
Jesus Is Our Light
LET'S CELEBRATE:
The Birth of Jesus

THE BLESSED BEATITUDES:
Sermon on the Mount

SERVICE WITH A SMILE:
Jesus Performed Miracles

CAPTAIN OF OUR SHIP:
Jesus Is Our Life Savior

Also supplement Primary Lessons and
Family Home Evenings with

# PRIMARY PARTNERS

starting with Nursery and Age 3 (Sunbeams)

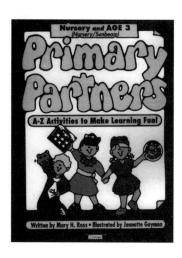

How do you teach a two-year old about feelings? Can you help a toddler to appreciate the scriptures? Does a three-year-old understand what it means to be reverent? You're already well on your way to the right answers with *Primary Partners*! Children will love the dozens of fun and unique crafts and activities contained in this book. And parents, nursery leaders, and Primary teachers will love the simple, creative, memorable ways in which even the youngest children can learn important gospel principles.

Each activity is listed alphabetically and cross-referenced to a particular lesson in the Primary 1 (Nursery and Age 3) manual.

With appealing artwork and fun-to-do games and crafts, *Primary Partners* is sure to be a hit with children. Use it every week in Primary, of course . . . but don't forget family home evening, where the good times get even better.

## Fun Activities to Help Your Little Ones Learn about the Gospel

- ♥ Example sandals to follow Jesus
- ♥ Moveable manger scene
- ♥ 3-D Noah's ark
- ♥ Ear-wings
- ♥ I Have "Bean" Obedient bean bag
- ♥ Tithing purse
- ♥ Bird watch
- ♥ Bug jar
- ♥ "Nature Walk" binoculars
- ♥ Giant eyes headband
- ♥ Fish bowl, fish and pole
- ♥ Smile and frown flip flag
- ♥ Hand-some bracelet
- ♥ Family face block
- ♥ Reverent church mouse maze
- ♥ Family prayer fan
- ♥ Temple tie and more . . .